WHAT I LEARNED FROM
MY THIRTY-DAY EUROPEAN ODYSSEY

ALSO BY M.P. PRABHAKARAN

Racist Bones in
President Trump's Body (2020)

An Indian Goes Around the World – I:
Capitalism Comes to Mao's Mausoleum (2012)

Letters on India The New York Times
Did Not Publish (2011)

The Historical Origin of India's Underdevelopment:
A World-System Perspective (1990)

WHAT I LEARNED FROM MY THIRTY-DAY EUROPEAN ODYSSEY

M. P. PRABHAKARAN

What I Learned from My Thirty-Day European Odyssey

This book is written to provide information and motivation to readers. Its purpose is not to render any type of psychological, legal, or professional advice of any kind. The content is the sole opinion and expression of the author, and not necessarily that of the publisher.

Copyright © 2021 by M. P. Prabhakaran.

All rights reserved. No part of this book may be reproduced, transmitted, or distributed in any form by any means, including, but not limited to, recording, photocopying, or taking screenshots of parts of the book, without prior written permission from the author or the publisher. Brief quotations for noncommercial purposes, such as book reviews, permitted by Fair Use of the U.S. Copyright Law, are allowed without written permissions, as long as such quotations do not cause damage to the book's commercial value. For permissions, write to the publisher, whose address is stated below.

Printed in the United States of America.

ISBN   978-1-953150-80-6   (Paperback)
ISBN   978-1-953150-81-3   (Digital)

Lettra Press books may be ordered through booksellers or by contacting:

Lettra Press LLC
30 N Gould St. Suite 4753
Sheridan, WY 82801
1 307-200-3414 | info@lettrapress.com
www.lettrapress.com

For the memory of my baby brother
RAMESH
*who passed away over half a century ago
at the tender age of five.
Hardly a day goes by, even now, when I don't think
about him, about the stories he told,
the songs he sang, the dances he danced… .*

Contents

Preface xi

CHAPTER

1 Sweet Memories of My First Visit Bring Me to Stockholm a Second Time 1

2 Chat with a Young Swedish Mother Married to an Iraqi Mechanic 7

3 Seeing Stockholm from the Water Is an Unforgettable Experience 12

4 From Stockholm to Helsinki, Pleasant Surprises All the Way 22

5 In the Land of the Midnight Sun, at the Peak of Summer 29

6 How Swedish-Russian Rivalry Affected Finland's Destiny 35

7 The Lesson I Learned from Three Russian Teenagers 41

8 St. Petersburg: How a Swamp Became the Cultural Capital of Russia 47

9 My Encounter with Russian Mafia on Busiest St. Petersburg Street 54

10 Catherine Palace and Peterhof: WWII Damage Still Being Repaired 59

11 Visit to Kazansky Cathedral; Date with Michelle; Chat with a Somali 65

12	How Three Russian Ladies Made My Journey to Moscow Pleasant and Easy	73
13	Tour of Kremlin and Red Square; a Crash Course in Moscow's History	80
14	Lovers and Newlyweds in Moscow Seal Their Bond with Padlocks	91
15	Two Uzbeks Greet Me with Song from Old Hindi Movie	98
16	Musings on How Baltic Breakaway Led to Soviet Breakup	104
17	Estonia's Capital Still Has an Old-World Charm	111
18	Tour of Latvian Capital; Lunch with a German-Thai Guilty of Being Rich	121
19	'Sitar Draws Out the Best in Me,' Says a German: My First Day in Warsaw	132
20	How I Celebrated the 65th Anniversary of Warsaw Uprising Against Nazis	138
21	Stalin's Gift to Polish People or Elephant in Lacy Underwear?	146
22	From Dubcek to Havel: A Mental Journey through Czech History	154
23	Tour of Prague, a City of Magnificent Monuments	160
24	Why Terezin Concentration Camp Was Called the Paradise Ghetto	168
25	A Sikh Victim of Khalistan Movement Happily Settled in Vienna	175
26	Visit to Austria's Melk Abbey; River Cruise Down the Danube	181
27	Flight to Frankfurt; Parting Gift from a German Fellow Passenger	186

28	Tamil Victim of Sri Lanka's Civil War Struggling to Make It in Frankfurt 193
29	What Frankfurt Was Like in Medieval Times............... 200
30	Flight from Frankfurt to Oslo, with Two Pakistani Sisters by My Side 209
31	Cruising through Oslo Fjord, and by Quisling's House 216
32	The More I Travel, the More I Discover My Ignorance 222

PICTURES

1	Once a Navy Ship, Now a Youth Hostel......................... 231
2	Monument to Birger Jarl 232
3	Changing of the Guard at Sweden's Royal Palace.......... 233
4	A Cruise Ship Leaving the Stockholm Harbor 234
5	The Lutheran Cathedral, Helsinki 235
6	The Statue of Three Blacksmiths 236
7	Statue of Havis Amanda 237
8	The Winter Palace, St. Petersburg 238
9	The Alexander Column in St. Petersburg........................ 239
10	The Catherine Palace, Pushkin 240
11	The Samson Fountain at Peterhof 241
12	Kazansky Cathedral, St. Petersburg 242
13	An Impromptu Dance Performance 243
14	Padlocks of Love on Trees of Love................................ 244
15	St. Basil's Cathedral in Red Square 245
16	The Kremlin Palace Complex.. 246
17	Tallinn, as Seen from the Cathedral Hill........................ 247
18	A Monument in Latvian Capital 248
19	Warsaw Uprising Memorial... 249

20	Stalin's Gift to Polish People	250
21	A Panoramic View of Prague	251
22	Statue of Madonna and St. Bernard on Charles Bridge	252
23	Astronomical Clock in Prague	253
24	Wachau Valley, as Seen from Melk Abbey	254
25	Farewell to Friends in Vienna	255
26	Frankfurt's Main Train Station	256
27	Euro Symbol, at ECB, Frankfurt	257
28	Cruising through the Oslo Fjord	258
29	Demand for Democracy in Iran	259
30	Statue of 'A Naked Family' in Oslo	260

Preface

This is the second book on my world-trotting experience. This one is devoted exclusively to the travels I undertook through 10 countries of Europe in the summer of 2009.

In the "Preface" to the first book, *Capitalism Comes to Mao's Mausoleum*, I expressed my passion for travel through a mangled version of the famous quote from the French philosopher Descartes: "I think, therefore I am." My mangled version: "I travel, therefore I am."

When I looked back at the end of my 30-day, 10-country European tour, another famous quote came to mind, this one from the 19th century English poet Percy Shelley: "The more we study, the more we discover our ignorance." A modified version of it aptly described what I felt at the end of the tour. My modified version: "The more I travel, the more I discover my ignorance."

I also said in the "Preface" to the first book: "Apart from being a source of great pleasure, traveling has also been my greatest learning experience in life... . I have a Ph.D. in Political Science from The New School for Social Research, New York. But what I learned from this prestigious American institution and, before that, from various academic institutions in India is no match for what I did from my travels around the world.

"The most valuable lesson I learned is that people are people – no matter what region or religion they belong to or what political system they live under. They open up to you if you approach them with an open mind."

The 2009 European tour proved to be a reaffirmation of those words. It convinced me, once again, that bookish knowledge is no substitute for the knowledge one gains from the people he interacts with and events and objects he gets exposed to during his travels to new places.

The tour opened my mind to various aspects of European cultures which I was quite ignorant of until then. It cleansed my mind of the many misconceptions I had about peoples and events that shaped the destiny of Europe.

My late journalist friend, Kulamarva Balakrishna, used to tell me: "What is the point in having knowledge, if you don't want to share it with others?" The main purpose of bringing out this book is to share with those who get to read it the knowledge I gained, and the joy I derived, from my 2009 European odyssey. Yes, it was nothing less than an odyssey.

>M.P. Prabhakaran
>Email address: prabha@eastwestinquirer.com
>or mprabhakaran@nyc.rr.com

1

Sweet Memories of My First Visit Bring Me to Stockholm a Second Time

July 15, 2009 – Wednesday

This was my second visit to Stockholm, the Swedish capital. Sweet memories of my first visit came back to me as I got off the plane, after an all-night flight from New York to Stockholm.

The first visit had been in the summer of 2008. I had arrived here by train from Oslo, the capital of Norway. I had arrived a day earlier than originally planned, and at an hour that any first-time visitor to a new place should avoid. The unplanned arrival happened because of a spur-of-the-moment decision I made while in Oslo: I decided to cut short my scheduled three-day stay in Oslo to two; utilize the one day thus saved to squeeze in a visit to Bergen, on the west coast of Norway; return to Oslo the next day; and then proceed to Stockholm, the next stop on my 2008 itinerary.

The belated decision to visit Bergen was made not because it is the second-largest city in Norway, but because of its reputation as being more beautiful than the largest, which is Oslo. There was one more reason, and a more important one: Most travel writers have said that an Oslo-to-Bergen, coast-to-coast train journey on a summer day is the best way to enjoy the scenic beauty of Norway.

I immensely enjoyed the train journey, all right. But my plan to stay overnight at Bergen fell through. The day of my arrival coincided with a much-publicized, open-air music concert by Eric Clapton, and all hotels, motels and hostels in the city had been booked weeks in advance. I had not known until then that the British rock star enjoyed that much popularity in Scandinavian countries. Disappointed, I took a train back to Oslo the same night.

Back in Oslo early the next morning, I was left with two options: spend one more day in Oslo or leave for Stockholm right away and add another day to my already-scheduled three-day stay in that city. I chose the latter.

I was hoping to take the train leaving Oslo at 7:30 a.m. It would bring me to Stockholm at 2 p.m., giving me sufficient time to search for a place to stay one night. My hope was dashed when I heard that the 7:30 train was fully booked. "Should I buy a ticket and get into an unreserved compartment?" I thought about it for a moment, and then decided against it. After an all-night travel from Bergen to Oslo, I was in no mood for another six-and-a-half-hour train journey, standing all the way. I bought a ticket for the next train to Stockholm, which was scheduled to leave Oslo at 3:38 p.m.

Little did I know at the time I bought the ticket that there was another disappointment awaiting me: Just two hours before the train was to depart, an announcement came on the station's PA system that all train services from Oslo up to Kongsvinger, a station in Norway close to the Swedish border, were canceled because of track work. The announcement also said that passengers would be transported by bus through the section affected by the cancellation. From Kongsvinger they could continue their journey, by train, to Stockholm.

Seated next to me on the bus from Oslo to Kongsvinger was a woman from the Philippines, who was working in Oslo. She worked for the Thon Hotel chain in Norway. When she heard from me that I was a little nervous about arriving in Stockholm around midnight and without any hotel reservation, she told me not to worry. "There is a youth hostel called af Chapman," she said. "Though a hostel, it's an exotic place. Part of it is an old ship permanently anchored and the other part, which is on the shore, is like any other hostel. Go check it out. The place is always sold out, especially in the summer. But there could be some last-minute cancellations. Try your luck. And it's only walking distance from the Stockholm Central Station, which will be your last stop."

She made the place more appealing when she said that she and her Swedish boyfriend had spent "some very interesting nights" there. (She had just been divorced from her Norwegian husband, marriage to whom was what brought her from the Philippines to Norway five years earlier.)

It was close to midnight by the time I reached the Stockholm Central Station. The Filipino woman had gotten off at the station before that. Because she had told me that the hostel was at walking distance from the station, I decided to walk, rather than take a taxi. Very soon I realized that the distance was too long to walk. Though Stockholm is one of the safest cities in the world, wandering around at midnight, in a strange city with no one in sight for blocks and blocks, would make any newly arrived person nervous. I enquired at a couple of bars on the way that were open and made sure that I was walking in the right direction.

After a good 45-minute walk, I reached the af Chapman hostel. And yet another disappointment was awaiting me there: "Every room at the hostel has been taken," the lady at the reception desk told me. On hearing from me that I was a total stranger to the city and sensing my nervousness about having to go around in the dead of night, looking for a place to stay, she and her colleague offered to help me. The colleague called up another facility, which happened to be another old ship converted into a hostel, and checked whether there was any vacancy there. I was relieved to hear that there was. He also called a taxi and told me how to get there and how much the approximate taxi fare would be. I was overwhelmed by the

Chapman staff's warmth and hospitality and their enthusiasm to help a stranger in distress. The distress instantly disappeared.

I remembered all that, as I walked in the arrival section of the Stockholm international airport, toward the immigration-clearance area. The tedium of the all-night flight from New York to Stockholm had already gone.

Tirade against President Bush

As the long line in front of the booths manned by immigration officials inched forward, another memorable experience I had during my 2008 visit came to mind: the conversation I had with a social worker during a subway ride in Stockholm. Marlene worked with children, ages 1 to 5, of newly arrived immigrants and refugees in Sweden. Working with the poor and helpless in the world was not just a job for her, she told me. It was her life's mission. "We Swedes must help others," I remembered her saying, "because we are in a position to do so." She also said that most people who needed help were in the desperate situation they were in for no fault of theirs. "Look at those coming from Iraq," she added. Then she launched a tirade against President George W. Bush and the American invasion of Iraq.

"I am glad that countries like Sweden opened their doors to refugees created by that invasion," I had told Marlene. "These countries could have easily said no. After all, they didn't create that problem."

"No," she had said, "we wouldn't say no to those helpless people. And we wouldn't allow our government to be that inhuman."

"I can vouch for that," I had replied. "In the couple of days I have been here, I was touched by the compassion and generosity of Swedes."

A rapport did develop between Marlene and me during our half-hour conversation. When the train arrived at the station where she had to get off, she said, "I would have enjoyed talking with you more, but for a commitment I have made to my friends." The commitment was "an evening out" with her girlfriends. "It's a girls-only party," she added. "Otherwise, I would have asked you to come along. We have the blessings of our boyfriends to go and enjoy."

"You have my blessing too," I told her. "Go and enjoy. Life is very short."

My mind was still with Marlene when my turn came to proceed to the immigration counter. Looking at my address in Sweden that I had written on the Immigration Form, the lady immigration officer said, "You have chosen a beautiful place to stay."

"I did it mainly for another reason," I told her. "I had a heart-warming experience with the staff at af Chapman last year." I briefly narrated the experience, and then added, "I had decided then and there that if I ever come back to Stockholm, and if I have to rent a place to stay, my first choice would be af Chapman." This time, I had booked the place weeks in advance.

The immigration officer stamped my passport and gave it back, saying, "Welcome to Stockholm." Just the kind of Swedish gesture I had expected. But what she said next surprised me: "Be careful about your wallet all the time. There are pickpockets around."

That was something I had not associated with Sweden. I said to myself: "This is the penalty a country pays for being so humane and generous toward the less fortunate in the world." Criminal elements from other countries have been sneaking into Sweden lately, taking advantage of that humanity and generosity.

I was still at the airport, now waiting at the carousel to pick up my checked-in bag. A larger-than-life picture on the wall caught my attention. It was the picture of a statue of Berger Jarl, the founder of Stockholm. The picture itself was more than sufficient to make anyone feel welcome to the city. So its caption that said, "Welcome to my hometown," was redundant.

I couldn't resist the urge to take a picture of that welcome sign. I looked around to see whether there was any security personnel nearby from whom I could take permission. I had to be cautious, airport security being overly strict since the 2001 terrorist attacks in the U.S. When I couldn't find anyone, I asked a man standing next to me, waiting for his baggage, whether there would be "any objection to my taking a picture of this."

"How long are you going to be in Stockholm?" he asked.

"Three days," I said.

"Go to the city hall one day," he said. "The statue of Berger Jarl that you are seeing in this picture is there in front of the city hall. Instead of taking a picture of a picture of the statue, why not take a picture of the statue itself?"

"Good suggestion," I told him and put my camera back into my pocket.

2

Chat with a Young Swedish Mother Married to an Iraqi Mechanic

July 16, 2009 – Thursday

I had set aside this day to take what is known in Stockholm as "the archipelago tour." My friends who had already taken this tour had talked about it in superlative terms. "It's an experience you will cherish all your life" – that's how some of them put it.

Most travel brochures I browsed said that the tour started in the morning at the Stockholm harbor and ended there in the evening. Which made me wonder: "How much of the Stockholm archipelago can a day's tour cover, given that it has thirty thousand islands and islets?" I was to learn later that the tour boats stop only at some of them. It's virtually impossible for any tour to cover all of the islands and islets in one day.

One of the islands all tour boats make it a point to stop at, and on which many tourists stay overnight, is Grinda Island. And that's the one I chose as the final stop on my archipelago tour. The day became memorable not just for the beauty of the island but, more importantly, for the wonderful conversation I had with a young Swedish mother on my way to it.

I had been told at the information desk at the Stockholm Central Station that I could save some money by boarding the boat to Grinda Island at Vaxholm, instead of Stockholm. The

72-hour, unlimited-ride metro pass that I had bought was good for the subway-cum-bus ride all the way from Stockholm to Vaxholm. The ride would take just two hours.

I was on the bus part of my journey to Vaxholm when, at the third stop, a young woman boarded the bus, cradling a tiny baby. She could be in her late teens or early twenties. I felt happy when she came and sat next to me, but also surprised when I took a good look at the baby. The baby appeared to be new-born, too tiny to be taken on a crowded bus. I couldn't help asking: "How old is this sweet little baby?"

"One month," the woman said.

My eyes nearly popped out. "Traveling on a crowded bus with your one-month-old baby?" I said. "You are really bold. Are you visiting your gynecologist?"

"No," she said. "My doctor took care of me only for a day. I stayed in the hospital only one day."

"And the doctor let you go just one day after the delivery?"

"I couldn't take it for more than a day. I couldn't sleep at all. I would have run away if the doctor had not allowed me to go."

"Is your mother taking care of you now?"

"No, I ran away from my mother long ago. We couldn't stand each other. She doesn't even know that I have a baby."

"So, who is helping you? Have you been doing everything by yourself from the second day of delivery? Does your husband help you with household chores?"

"Are you kidding? In his culture, the wife is supposed to do everything. He is from Iraq."

"Is he a practicing Muslim?" I asked.

"No. He told me that he was very religious before he came to this country. That was ten years ago. Now he drinks and does all sorts of things."

I didn't want to appear too nosy. So I didn't ask her what she meant by "all sorts of things." If he came to Sweden 10 years earlier, I surmised, he was not one of the victims of the American invasion of Iraq. He might have left Iraq because he was unhappy under Saddam Hussein's dictatorship. I wanted to know more. On second thoughts, I decided to let that touchy political subject also pass. But I was keen on continuing the conversation with the young mother who was open-minded enough to have an Iraqi husband.

"Have you heard about Ramadan?" I asked her.

"Yes," she said.

"It's an important month for Muslims. Even the not-so-religious among them fast during Ramadan. Does your husband do it?"

"No. I wish he had done it. He is very fat. Fasting would do him a lot of good."

I decided to change the subject. "People usually go to Vaxholm to take a boat to one of the nearby islands," I said. "Are you on such a trip with your one-month-old baby?"

Vaxholm Ice Cream

"No, Vaxholm is also known for good ice cream. I am going to meet my girlfriend there. We'll have some ice cream, walk around a bit and I go back home this evening. I hope Emilia doesn't give me a hard time."

The mention of her daughter's name made me realize that I had not told her my name. I did it, and added, "I am sorry. I should have introduced myself before asking all those personal questions."

"That's OK," she said. "My name is Sanno."

"Couldn't Emilia's father join you on this ice cream-eating expedition?" I asked.

"He said he had to work today. 'In that case, I will go alone,' I told him. That's the one thing I like about him: He takes his work seriously. He is a self-employed mechanic. He repairs and retrofits old cars and trucks and sells them. He is doing OK as a small businessman."

By then, the bus had arrived at Vaxholm. Sanno's friend was waiting at the bus-stop. She was cuddling a poodle. After Sanno introduced me to her, I almost blurted out, "Couldn't you have an Emilia to cuddle, as your friend Sanno is doing?" I was prudent enough to control my tongue and ask a different question: "Are you fond of ice cream too?"

"Yes, very much," she said. And, giving a pat on Sanno's shoulder, she added, "Actually, that's one of the things that bonded us."

"Enjoy your ice cream," I told her. Turning to Sanno, I said, "I wish you and Emilia all the best. Don't forget to tell her, once she is grown up enough to understand, that you got out of the hospital just one day after giving birth to her."

I shook hands with the two ladies and watched them walk away, Sanno cradling Emilia and her friend still cuddling her poodle.

It seemed that the animated conversation I was having with a total stranger on the bus had caught the attention of the bus-driver. He was standing beside the bus, getting ready for his return trip, when I passed by him. He smiled at me and said, "I am sure the lady was telling you something very interesting. What's it all about?"

"I can't believe what I heard from her," I told the driver. "She is a wonder woman. She tells me that she stayed in the hospital only one day after giving birth to the baby. In India, no doctor would ever allow a woman to do that. In the U.S., the fear of mal-practice suits alone prevents doctors from doing it. And she says she has no help from her mother or anyone else in taking care of the baby or doing household work."

"I am not surprised by the first part," the driver said. "My mother stayed in the hospital only for two days after giving birth to me. But the second part – not getting any help from mother or anyone else after childbirth – that's rare even in Sweden."

"Sweden is known for its excellent medical care," I said. "I also know it's free. In spite of that, people are reluctant to stay in hospitals? I find it odd."

I told the bus-driver about the tradition in India of mothers moving in with their daughters during childbirth and staying on at least a few days thereafter. "I am told that for young women, their mothers are of great help in getting over the postpartum depression," I said. "This lady says she and her mother can't stand each other. Her mother doesn't even know that she has a baby."

"That's rare too," the driver said. "But then, there are broken families all over the world."

"Absolutely true," I told him. "I didn't mean to give you the impression that family relationships in India are perfect. There are rotten things happening there also. I just mentioned a tradition that existed."

"Time for me to go," the driver said and got on the bus.

3

Seeing Stockholm from the Water Is an Unforgettable Experience

July 17, 2009 – Friday

"If you're looking to see Stockholm from the water, this is the tour for you." When I read the line, written in bold letters on a banner in front of one of the stalls at the Stockholm harbor, I thought it was specially meant for me. I had been looking forward to taking such a tour ever since I heard that seeing Stockholm from its lakes and canals was an unforgettable experience.

Apart from enabling one to enjoy the beauty of Stockholm's skyline, the tour takes him through parts of the city which he otherwise would bypass. But for the two-hour tour that I took, I wouldn't have known what an inner city in Stockholm looked like. I wouldn't have known how beautiful the islands of Södermalm, Lilla Essingen and Stora Essingen, and the green areas of Djurgarden are. Thanks to the tour, I now know why city planners from around the world are flocking to Hammarby Sjöstad (roughly translated as Hammarby Lake City). It is a bellwether for eco-conscious, eco-friendly city planning.

When I bought the ticket for the tour, entitled "Under the Bridges of Stockholm," I knew it was unrealistic to expect the boat to go under all the bridges in the city. They are too numerous to cover in two hours. The boat passed under 15 bridges and the locks that connect Lake Mälaren to the Baltic Sea.

Until this tour, I had only heard and read about water locks that facilitate passage of vessels from one body of water to another. This was the first time that I watched how a lock worked.

How a Water Lock Works

A lock is a man-made, rectangular chamber, with gates at both ends, that connects two bodies of water. The water level, as we all know, varies from lake to lake, river to river and sea to sea. When a vessel enters a lock, the water inside the lock is at the same level as the body of water it has just left. Once the vessel is inside the lock, the gate through which it has just entered the lock shuts from behind. Once the vessel is locked in, the level of water inside the lock is raised or lowered, by pumping water into or out of it, to bring it to the same level as the next body of water the vessel is going to enter. Once that is done, the gate of the lock in front of the vessel opens, and the vessel enters the new body of water – lake, river or sea. Being my first exposure to how the lock mechanism worked, I watched it with great enthusiasm. (To get slightly ahead of the story, I was less enthusiastic when, three years later, I watched how the three locks in the Panama Canal connecting the Atlantic and Pacific Oceans worked, though the lock mechanism in the latter is much more advanced.)

As the boat passed by important landmarks in Stockholm, I noted them down, hoping to visit some of them on my own at the end of the tour. The pre-recorded commentary on the boat, which provided interesting pieces of information on the Swedish society, history and politics, was very helpful in deciding which ones to visit.

As we passed by an old ship used by the Vikings, which is now a restaurant, the commentary dwelt at some length on the Viking era in the Scandinavian history – the era in which

Scandinavian coasts were frequently subjected to exploration and plunder by the Vikings. Just by coincidence, a luxury cruise ship sailed by us, which had "The Viking Line" written on its side in bold, attractive letters. It was on its way to Helsinki. Looking at the beautiful ship, I found it difficult to associate the Vikings with plunder. The Viking Line is one of the companies that regularly transport passengers, most of them fun-seeking vacationers, between Stockholm and Helsinki.

When the boat sailed by the Vasa Museum, the commentary switched to the history of another ship and to how it became a museum piece. The Vasa ship was added to the Royal Swedish Navy, on August 10, 1628, with great fanfare. Alas, it remained part of the navy only for a few minutes after its launch! It had sailed on its maiden voyage just about 1,300 meters, when, in a light gust of wind, it capsized and sank. For Sweden, it was a major national disaster. Not just because it claimed 53 lives, but because it was the most expensive project the country had undertaken until then. More important, at the time of the disaster, the country was at war with Poland and it badly needed the ship in its war efforts.

The Vasa was more or less forgotten about for over three centuries. It was relocated in 1956 by a man by the name of Anders Franzen. In 1961, 333 years after it sank, it was raised to the surface. Today, it is housed in the Vasa Museum, near the site where it foundered.

When the commentary on the ill-fated Vasa ship was over, I said to a fellow tourist, "Now I know that the Titanic was not the only expensive, highly decorated ship that sank on its maiden voyage."

"Absolutely true," he replied.

When the commentary gave interesting tidbits on the Royal Palace, the Royal Swedish Opera House and the city hall, I said to myself that I should visit them before the day was over. As soon as the boat tour ended, a little after 11 a.m., I headed to the Royal Palace. It's only walking distance from where we were.

The Royal Palace

The Royal Palace of Stockholm is one of the largest palaces in Europe. It was built, as the King of Sweden's official residence, on the spot where the Tre Kronor Castle once stood. The Tre Kronor Castle, named for the three golden crowns that decorated its tower, burned down in a devastating fire, on May 7, 1697. The golden crowns are Sweden's national coat of arms. Though the construction of the palace began soon after the fire, it was completed only in 1754. The Great Northern War, which marked the beginning of Sweden's decline as a superpower in the Baltic region, interrupted the work. Adolf Frederick was the first Swedish king to occupy the newly-built palace.

Now the King of Sweden uses the Royal Palace only for official purposes. He lives elsewhere and comes there to work every day. The palace draws large crowds of tourists throughout the day, especially in the summer.

A daily event at the palace, which all tourists are advised not to miss, is the Changing of the Guard. It takes place at 12:15 p.m. (On Sundays, it does at 1:15 p.m.) As I entered the palace gate, I saw a throng of tourists jostling for vantage positions to watch the event. I jostled with them too. The spectacular show is presented by the palace guards picked for the day's duty. They are picked from the 30,000-strong Royal Guard, which in turn is drawn from Sweden's armed forces.

After watching the 40-minute ceremony, I wandered around the palace. Few visitors will have the time and patience to go through all the 600 rooms, many of them fabulously decorated, of the vast complex. But none would want to miss the most important ones, the ones that are steeped in history. I visited some of them.

The first one was the Gallery of Charles XI. This was the place where Charles XI held state receptions and dinners. According to a travel brochure I had with me, this room was modeled on the famous mirror room in the Versailles Palace. Having visited the Versailles Palace a few years ago, I could say that the claim was justifiable.

Another famous room in the palace is the Rikssalen (the State Room). Its silver throne, built in 1650 for the coronation of Queen Christina, was one of the few items salvaged from the 1697 fire.

The royal chapel in the palace, decorated in Rococo style by Carl Hårleman, is a big tourist draw. It was consecrated in 1754.

History buffs among tourists would find some of the museums in the palace fascinating. The Tre Kronor Museum recreates the palace's medieval history. The few objects, other than the silver throne, recovered from the ruins of the Tre Kronor Castle are displayed in this museum.

Gustav III, the king of Sweden from 1771 to 1792, was reputed to be "a vigorous patron of the arts." The Gustav III Antikmuseum bears evidence to that reputation. Among the items on display in it are several statues, which the king had brought from Rome.

The Livrustkammaren (the Royal Armory) has a collection of armor, carriages and costumes that the royalty used in the medieval period. And the Skattkammaren (the Treasure Chamber) displays the crown jewels and other treasures of the period. One of the treasures is the sword of King Gustav Vasa.

Unlike most palaces in Europe and Asia, admission to the Royal Palace of Sweden is free. At the end of my 2008 trip to Stockholm, I had left the city with one regret: that I had failed to visit the Royal Palace. Not many tourists have made that mistake. This time, as I came out of the palace gate, I realized what I had actually missed in 2008.

The Royal Opera House

My next destination was the Royal Opera House. It's a few minutes' walk from the palace, and connected to it by a bridge.

This magnificent neoclassical building, designed by Axel Anderberg and opened in 1898, is an extension of the Royal

Palace in terms of grandeur. It was meant to be that way, we were told. After walking by its front façade adorned with statues, arches and columns; through its 92-foot-long Golden Foyer decorated with crystal chandeliers and ceiling paintings by Carl Larsson; and up the marble staircase leading to a three-tiered, chandeliered auditorium that can seat 1200 people, we could see that designer Anderberg had taken great care to blend the opera house well with the nearby palace, architecturally.

At the end of the tour of this majestic building, walking through its Golden Foyer once again, I thought about the man who founded the Swedish opera and the fate that befell him on the spot where I was standing. The man was King Gustav III.

As mentioned above, he was a great patron of the arts. One of the arts he patronized was opera. He also commissioned the construction of the first opera house in Sweden. Named after him, the Gustavianska Operahuset (the Gustavian Opera House) was opened in 1782.

Little did he know then that 10 years later, the house he built to promote the art he loved would be the scene of his own assassination. The assassination had nothing to do with the art, though. It had to do with a trait in his personality that angered some in the political arena. They found him despotic.

Though despotic, some of the reforms he introduced in the country – like abolition of torture as an instrument of legal investigation and religious tolerance – earned him the adulation of the masses. But one 'reform,' the one that increased the power of the royalty at the expense of the Riksdag (Sweden's parliament), alienated him from a section of the nobility in the country. A conspiracy grew out of that alienation. One of the conspirators, Captain Jacob Johan Anckarström, shot him point-blank, when he was enjoying a masquerade ball in the foyer of the very opera house he built ten years earlier. The shooting took place on March 16, 1792, and he passed away 13 days later.

The Gustavian Opera House was demolished in 1891. The one we see now, built on the same spot, was inaugurated in

1898 by King Oscar II with a performance of Franz Berwald's *Estrella de Soria*.

While leaving the opera house, my thoughts were on Gustav III the art-lover, not Gustav III the despot. I walked toward the next stop I had marked for a visit: the Stockholm City Hall.

Visit to the City Hall

I had read somewhere that the Stockholm City Hall was built to look like a swan resting on water. From the angle from which I approached it, it did look like a swan – with some stretch of imagination, of course. And I didn't have time to try and find what it looked like from other angles. I am not trying to belittle the grandeur of what is said to be "one of the country's leading examples of national romanticism in architecture." An important center of Stockholm's political, cultural and social life, it certainly is impressive and imposing.

The three golden crowns on the spire atop the city hall's 106-meter-tall tower shone brighter in the evening sun. One piece of art, which none approaching the city hall would fail to notice, is the statue of Birger Jarl, mounted on a tall pillar. It looks as if the man acclaimed to be the founder of Stockholm were welcoming those approaching the city from afar.

Once inside the building, I was a little disappointed to learn that certain areas were open to the public only through guided tours. As it was well past the time for the last guided tour, I decided to wander around and explore things on my own. There were a lot to explore.

There is a monument to Birger Jarl inside the city hall too. It is in the form of an empty coffin, with the dead body of Birger Jarl placed on top of it. Both the coffin and the body are cast in bronze, with a gold coating on it.

Jarl is a title in the ruling hierarchy of Sweden, next only to that of king. Birger wielded tremendous power in Sweden, not only by virtue of his being a jarl but also because of his marriage to King Eric XI's sister. On King Eric's death, in 1250, in accordance with the matrilineal system that prevailed in the country at the time, Birger's son, the king's nephew, became the ruler of the country. But because the son was a minor, Birger acted as his regent. That is, Birger Jarl was the virtual ruler of Sweden from 1250 until his death, on October 1, 1266. (The exact date of his birth is unknown. Historians have placed the year of birth at 1210.)

Another thing about Birger Jarl that is in dispute is the claim that he was the founder of Stockholm. What is not in dispute, however, is that he "made the country more civilized by enacting [among other things] laws that protected the rights of women," according to *Encyclopedia Britannica*.

Apart from housing various departments of the city administration, the Stockholm City Hall also serves as the venue of the great Nobel banquet. It is held annually on December 10, at the end of the ceremony conferring Nobel Prizes. The Nobel Prizes, as we know, are conferred by four institutions – three of them Swedish and one Norwegian. The Royal Swedish Academy of Sciences confers the prizes in physics, chemistry and economics; the Karolinska Institute, in physiology or medicine; and the Swedish Academy (different from the Royal Swedish Academy), in literature. The prize for peace is conferred by the Norwegian Nobel Committee, based in Oslo, and the prize-giving ceremony is held at the Oslo City Hall.

The prize-giving ceremony in Sweden, held at the Stockholm Concert Hall, is followed by a banquet at the Stockholm City Hall. In addition to the Nobel laureates and their families, the king and queen and other members of the royal family of Sweden are guests of honor at both the award ceremony and the banquet. I passed by the Blue Hall where they all dine and the Golden Hall where they – i.e., those who want to – dance.

An Enterprising News Vendor

As I came out of the city hall, I was pleasantly surprised to see on the sidewalk a news vendor who had several English newspapers displayed on a makeshift newsstand. The newsstand was mounted on a wheelbarrow, which was attached to a van.

Since morning, I had been looking for a copy of *The International Herald Tribune*. For a *New York Times* addict, it is the next best thing, when he is in Europe. I jumped for joy when the vendor said that he had both, but in a slightly different format. He had all leading English and French dailies, photocopied page-for-page from the original, and stapled.

"Are you not violating copyright laws?" I asked him.

"No," he said. "I have an arrangement with all these publications to do what I am doing." He pointed at the framed permit hung in front of the wheelbarrow.

He said he was originally from London, now living in Prague. "I have a regular job in Prague," he added. "I do this on the side. The man who works for me here is on vacation. So I flew in to fill in for him."

"Very enterprising," I told him.

"An enterprising person can always create jobs for himself," he said, "no matter the slump in the economy."

When I told him that I would be in Prague the next month, he gave me some tips on the places I must visit while there. "This is one of the few advantages of traveling alone," I said. "You can stop where and when you want to and chat with whomsoever you want to." I shook hands with him and thanked him for the tips.

It was past 6 p.m., and I was in no mood to call it a day. There was one more reason why: it was my last day in Stockholm and I wanted to enjoy the sights and sounds of the city as long as my energy level permitted. I continued my wandering.

Sri Chinmoy Peace Capital

After several minutes of aimless wandering, I reached a place called the Cultural Centre. A plaque placed on a concrete slab in front of one of the buildings at the place caught my attention. Actually, it was not the plaque, but the message inscribed on it, that did it. The message is from the late Sri Chinmoy, whose career I had followed fairly closely.

He was born in East Bengal (now Bangladesh) in 1931 and died in New York on October 11, 2007. Since he moved to New York on April 13, 1964, it had been his home. With New York as base, this Aurobindo Ashram-trained Indian guru traveled around the world to spread his message, the essence of which is:

"Our goal is to go from bright to brighter to brightest, from high to higher to highest. And even in the highest, there is no end to our progress, for God Himself is inside each of us and God at every moment is transcending His own Reality."

I was pleasantly surprised to see that Sweden was one of the 60 countries in which the Indian mystic had won disciples. I don't know whether it was his Swedish disciples' idea to call Stockholm "A Sri Chinmoy Peace Capital." The inscription on the plaque does it.

The main Chinmoy message, inscribed on September 10, 1998, reads:

> Good it is
> To receive peace in the world.
> Better it is
> To give peace to the world.
> Best, by far the best, it is
> To become the peace of the world.

The message echoed in my mind the rest of the evening. "What better way to end my visit to Stockholm, where I have had the good fortune to be a beneficiary of the best in Swedes," I said to myself while retiring to bed.

4

From Stockholm to Helsinki, Pleasant Surprises All the Way

July 18, 2009 – Saturday

I was on my way to Helsinki. When I left af Chapman hostel early in the morning, I was not expecting to see what I did on the waterfront outside: more than half a dozen photographers, in lying position, training their cameras on I didn't know what. Another half-dozen or so were walking about, with tripods and cameras in their hands, looking for the right positions from which to photograph, again, I didn't know what.

The amusing part of the spectacle was that those who were in lying position were so engrossed in their work that they were oblivious to what their low-waist jeans failed to cover. Parts of their buttocks were exposed, cleavage and all. There was no mistaking that all these men were professional photographers.

Suppressing the laugh which the exposed parts of their anatomies had evoked in me, I approached one of the men and asked, "What is this about?"

"Oh," he said, "we are going to send these pictures as entries in an international photo competition being held in New York. The topic of the competition is 'Cities around the World.' All of us are trying to get the best shot of what Stockholm looks like on a summer morning."

My Thirty-Day European Odyssey

It was a beautiful morning. Though not 5 a.m. yet, the sun had already risen. Remember, we are talking about the Land of the Midnight Sun. The yellow buildings on the western shore of the canal looked yellower in the morning sun. Their reflection in the placid waters of the canal was beautiful to watch. Maybe that was what the photographers were trying to capture with their cameras.

"All of you are so dedicated to your profession," I told the man. Though I had the bare bottoms of his fellow competitors for proof, I didn't mention it. "The city is hardly awake," I added, "and you are already on the job. I will be in New York in a month from now. I am going to find out more about this competition when I get there. I hope you win a prize. Wish you all the best."

Mix-up about the Bus Schedule

I headed for the nearby bus-stop. I was hoping to catch the first bus going in the direction of the train station. The first bus, as I had noted the day before, was scheduled to leave at 5 a.m. About five minutes' ride would take me to the Stockholm Central Station. The metro ride from there to a city called Marsta would take an hour; and another bus ride, from Marsta to the Stockholm Arlanda Airport, would take another 10 minutes. Taking into account that I was traveling on a weekend, that too early in the morning, I had provided for some extra time. Thus, after a leisurely travel by public transportation, I was hoping to reach the airport around 7 a.m. My flight to Helsinki was scheduled to depart at 8:35 a.m.

But things did not turn out the way I had planned. It was several minutes past 5 a.m., and there was no sign of any bus. "It's not like Sweden," I said to myself. Sweden and other Scandinavian countries are known for their punctuality. I took another look at the bus schedule. How stupid of me! What I had noted down yesterday was the weekday schedule. On weekends, the first bus leaves only at 8 a.m.

It was to meet eventualities like this that I added extra time to the actual travel time. I started walking toward the train station. I knew it would take only less than half an hour if I walked fast. The company of a pretty young woman made the walk enjoyable.

She was snapping the same scene that the other photographers I had seen doing a few minutes earlier. When she finished the snapping, I asked her what the shortest route to the train station was.

"Follow me," she said. We walked side by side.

"Are you also participating in the photo competition?" I asked her.

"What photo competition?" she said. "I haven't even heard about it." She was taking pictures for her own pleasure.

"In that case," I said, "hum, let me guess: you just came out of that jazz festival."

An all-night, five-night-long international jazz festival was going on in Stockholm at that time.

"No," she said, "it is too expensive for me. Two thousand kronor for five nights or five hundred kronor for one night. That's way beyond a sales assistant's budget for pleasure."

"Actually, that's why I didn't attend it, though I love jazz," I told her. "It's way beyond the budget of a frugal traveler."

"I am not a jazz fan anyway," she said. "I enjoy dancing. For two hundred kronor, I was able to dance the night away with my friends, at an inexpensive nightclub in the Old Town." She pointed to the hilly area on the other side of the canal.

We talked about many more things – music, places we two had visited in Europe etc. – and kept walking. When we reached the front of a store, opposite the Stockholm Central Station, she stopped. "This is where I work," she said, pointing to the shuttered store. "It will be open at nine o' clock. Today is my day off. I sell world maps here."

"You can be a good tour guide," I told her.

"Yes, I thought about it," she said. "Apart from Swedish and, as you know by now, English, I speak French. Yes, I can be a tour guide for English- and French-speaking tourists."

"Think about it seriously. You will make an excellent tour guide," I said.

We shook hands and said good-bye to each other. I crossed the road and walked toward the train station. I was feeling ecstatic that the day started so pleasantly, a few minutes' frustration over the bus schedule mix-up notwithstanding.

On the train, two seats away from me, a young man, 20-something, was jabbering away on his cellphone, in Bengali. He looked like someone heading home after all-night work. I took him to be a Bangladeshi. Most of the South-Asian-looking people I came across, during my three days in Stockholm, were from either Bangladesh or Pakistan.

I reached the airport a few minutes before 7 a.m. I was about to approach the check-in counter when an announcement came from the airline that our flight was overbooked. Those who volunteered to take the next flight, which would be three hours later, would receive a compensation of 300 euros, the announcement said.

Arriving in Helsinki three hours later wouldn't make much difference to an aimless wanderer like me. And the compensation offered was tempting. I decided to volunteer. But when I approached the announcer and was told that the compensation would be in the form of a voucher for future travels, I changed my mind. "I want cash or cashier's check," I told her.

Meeting with My Finnish Friend

It was 10:30 a.m. by the time I arrived at the hostel in Helsinki, where I had booked a room. The first thing I did after checking in was call Martine (not her real name). That was the promise I had given her. "Please don't waste your time coming to the airport to fetch me," I had told her over the phone before leaving New York. "I will find my way to the hostel."

Since I met Martine and her mother in Berlin the year before, we had been in touch with each other through email. The casual acquaintance between Martine and me, which began in Berlin, had developed into a close friendship.

Martine came over to the hostel in the afternoon. We spent the rest of the day wandering around Helsinki. The first place she took me to was the Olympics stadium. Helsinki had hosted the Summer Olympics in 1952.

In front of the stadium stands a statue of Lauri Tahko Pihkala (1888-1981). Pihkala became famous as a Finnish sportsman, but not through his performance at the two Summer Olympics he participated in: In 1908, he was only 16th in the high-jump competition; and in 1912, in the 800-meter run, he was eliminated in the first round itself.

His invaluable contribution to Finland's sports came in the form of a game he invented: *pesapallo*, which is the Finnish variant of baseball. For that, and for developing several other games in Finland, he was awarded an honorary doctorate in sport sciences by the University of Jyvaskyla, in 1969. Though his right-wing political activism had earned him the wrath of many of his countrymen, they were willing to condone it because of his achievements in the field of sports.

Paavo Nurmi

On another side of the stadium stands another statue, that of the legendary Finnish athlete Paavo Nurmi (1897-1973). It was sculpted by Wäinö Aaltonen. Nurmi was one of the most successful male athletes in the history of the Olympics and one of only four to win nine Olympic gold medals. He won them in cross-country; 10,000-meter; 5,000-meter; and 3,000-meter races at three consecutive Olympics: Antwerp (1920); Paris (1924); and Amsterdam (1928). He had also won three silver medals – one at Antwerp and two at Amsterdam. Of the nine gold medals he won, three were at Antwerp, five at Paris and one was at Amsterdam. He was one of the group of Finnish athletes nicknamed the "Flying Finns."

From the stadium, Martine drove me to Senate Square, which is considered "the monumental center of Helsinki." The man credited with bringing that distinction to the place was the famous German architect, Carl Ludvig Engel (1778-1840). He was tasked with rebuilding Helsinki, which had been nearly destroyed in the wars between Sweden and Russia. Finland, it may be added, was ruled by Sweden from 1155 to 1809. After the 1808-1809 war between Sweden and Russia, which was known as the "Finnish War," it came under Russian rule and became the Grand Duchy of Russia. It remained so until 1917, the year in which Finland declared its independence.

Among the buildings in Senate Square that bear the impress of Engel's architectural style – known as the "Empire Style" – are the Senate (which is now the Palace of the Council of State); the library and the main building of Helsinki University; and the Helsinki Cathedral (also known as the Lutheran Cathedral).

The Lutheran Cathedral, which is an imposing structure, was built over a period of 22 years, from 1830 to 1852. Engel oversaw its construction until his death in 1840, when it was taken over by Ernst Lohrmann. The latter did make some additions to Engel's design: statues in zinc of the Twelve Apostles placed on the roof of the cathedral, a bell tower and a side chapel. It underwent further renovations in 1998. Now, it is one of the main tourist attractions in Helsinki, receiving more than 350,000 visitors a year.

The cathedral was built as a tribute to Nicholas I, the czar of Russia from 1825 to 1855. Until 1917, the year of Finland's independence from Russia, it was called St. Nicholas Church. It became a cathedral of the Evangelical Lutheran denomination only in 1959.

Father of Literary Finnish

The evangelical who brought Protestant Reformation – more specifically, Lutheranism – to Finland was Michael Agricola (1510-1557). Consecrated as the bishop of Turku (Abo) in Sweden in 1554, he had a falling out with the pope, which led to his reforming the Finnish Church along Lutheran lines. The Finnish Church, at the time, was part of the Church of Sweden.

Agricola had his early lessons in Lutheranism under no less a person than the founder of the movement himself. Martin Luther, the founder, was an instructor at the University of Wittenberg, Germany, when Agricola was a student there, from 1536 to 1539. He also lived at Luther's home during that period.

It was Michael Agricola who first translated the New Testament into Finnish. He also produced the prayer book and hymns used in Finland's new Lutheran churches. He was called the "father of literary Finnish," because it was his work that set the rules of orthography that are the basis of modern Finnish spelling.

It was a bright, sunny evening, and the streets were crowded. Martine and I decided to hang around *Keskusta/Centrum* for some more time before calling it a day. Both *Keskusta* in Finnish and *Centrum* in Swedish mean the center. In this case, the street sign refers to the city center. Most place names and street names in Helsinki are written in Finnish and Swedish. That is, the vestiges of Finland's having once been ruled by Sweden still linger. They linger even two centuries after its independence from Sweden.

Martine was not proud of the Swedish past – and the Russian past – in her country's history. I figured it out from the way she referred to the bilingual road signs all over Helsinki. "Tourists would have found it helpful if they had written them in English too," she remarked a couple of times.

5

In the Land of the Midnight Sun, at the Peak of Summer

July 19, 2009 – Sunday

When I met Martine and her mother in Berlin in the summer of 2008, I had told them about a desire I had been nurturing for some time: to experience what it is like being in Finland at the height of summer and winter. Finland being part of the Land of the Midnight Sun, its summer nights are very, very short. In the Lapland area of the country, it is virtually day all 24 hours, at least in two summer months. The sun may disappear briefly at what the clock says is midnight, but the sunlight lingers. In the winter, on the other hand, one rarely sees the sun. It is grayish even at noon.

"For you two, this phenomenon may be a reality of life," I had told Martine and her mother. "For me, it's only bookish knowledge. One day, before I kick the bucket, I want to make it a real-life experience."

"You must," the mother had said. "Whether there is sun or not, people go about doing their things, as in any other part of the world. We want you to find it out for yourself."

While wandering around with Martine on this sunny July Sunday in Helsinki, I told her, "Remember what I had told you and Mom last year? About my wanting to be in Finland at the peaks of summer and winter?"

"Yes, I remember."

"Right now, I am fulfilling the first part of my wish. I don't know when I am going to do the second part. Be prepared for the boredom you will have to suffer when it happens."

"You can come here any number of times, in any season," Martine responded. "As long as I am here, you will have a friend to go around with." I was touched by the response.

There's one more thing about Martine that left a deep impression on me: A Finnish Lutheran, she is married to a Moroccan Muslim. There is nothing special about that, you may say. But there is more to that relationship.

An Unusual Love Story

Martine is a college graduate who knows five languages. The man she married is a high school dropout. His mother tongue is Arabic. When they met, he spoke no Finnish but knew a little French, which Martine is fluent in. At the time they met, he was making a living as an undocumented manual laborer in Helsinki. She was a graduate student majoring in graphic design.

When she told her college buddies that she was going to marry this guy, they thought she was crazy. "What do you see in him?" some of them had asked her. She told them all to get lost.

I had patted Martine on her back when she narrated her love story while in Berlin the year before. Her Muslim husband also had won my admiration when she told me that not once had he or anyone from his family asked her to convert to Islam. Since they met, she had visited his family in Morocco twice.

I had been looking forward to meeting him and was disappointed when Martine said that he couldn't join us. "He has to work," she said. "He is painting somebody's apartment. He had promised the apartment owner that he would complete it today. His work ethic is another thing that I admire in him."

"Please tell your husband that I admire it too," I told Martine. "Let him know that I am anxious to meet him one day."

I had not told Martine, but she knew, that her being in Helsinki was the second reason why I put the city on my itinerary this time. (The first was my obsession mentioned above.) She had decided to do everything she could to make my three days in the city as comfortable as possible.

"You are lucky that both yesterday and today happened to be unusually sunny," she said. "Unusual for Helsinki, I mean. It was raining all last week."

"Pardon my sounding conceited," I replied. "The sunny days have something to do with my arrival. Will I be boring you if I continue?"

"I will tell you when you do," she said. "Please continue."

"In my mother tongue, the word *Prabhakaran* means one who creates light. It's a synonym for the sun. The sun is one of the gods in Hindu mythology."

She gave me a pat on my shoulder. "That's why I love traveling," she said. "I wouldn't have got this information if I had not met you."

"And I wouldn't have had the tons of non-bookish knowledge about Finland if I had not met you," I said.

Then she changed the topic. Pointing to the huge clock at the main entrance to the Stockmann Department Store, the largest department store in Helsinki, she said, "This spot is a popular rendezvous for us Helsinkians. Friends would simply say, Let's meet at the clock."

A few yards away from Stockmann is the *Statue of Three Blacksmiths*. We walked toward it. Made possible by a donation from the businessman Julius Tallberg, and sculpted by Felix Nylund, the statue shows three naked, muscular men hammering on an anvil. It was donated to the city by the Pro Helsingfors Foundation in 1932. According to a story the Finns enjoy telling visitors, the blacksmiths will strike the anvil whenever a virgin walks by.

"Why aren't they striking now?" I asked Martine. "Do you mean to say that not one of these girls is a virgin?" I added, pointing to a group of young girls who just passed by the statue.

"Come on," Martine said, "you have heard such stories all over the world." She nudged me to move on.

After wandering for a few more minutes, we ambled into an open-air bar.

The pleasant conversation we were having over a beer was interrupted and spoiled by the boisterousness of three drunken men sitting at a nearby table. One of the two ladies sitting next to us asked me whether I was from India. When I replied yes, she said, "I will be flying to Islamabad, Pakistan, tomorrow." The trip had to do with the work she was doing for an NGO. She didn't tell me the name of the NGO, and I didn't ask either. She was a little apprehensive about "flying to one of the trouble spots in the world."

"Don't worry," I told her, "you will be all right."

Alcoholism, a Major Problem

After a few minutes' chat, I handed her my camera and requested that she take a picture of me and Martine. Hardly had she taken one picture when one of the drunken men came and stood behind us. He placed his hands on our shoulders, almost knelt to bring his face to the same level as ours, and insisted that a picture be taken of the three of us together. We didn't know what gesture he made with his face. It did make his two friends burst out into loud laughs. The lady, who was still holding my camera, obliged him. While handing the camera back to me, she whispered, "Delete it when you reach home."

But the drunken man was in no mood to leave us alone. Now he wanted to know: "Where did my little princess meet this ugly foreigner?"

At that point, Martine took my hand and said, "Come, let's go."

As we walked out, she threw a contemptuous look at the man. The two ladies who were sitting next to us bowed their heads in shame and buried their faces in their hands.

"I am ashamed of my countrymen when they behave like this," Martine said.

"Don't feel embarrassed," I told her. "Every country has characters like these."

"Alcoholism is a major problem in our country," she said. "So are alcohol-related deaths. I think I had told you about my father."

"Yes, you had."

"He was a World War Two veteran. He drank himself to death. My mother walked out on him when his drinking got out of control. Now she lives with her friend. Can I call a man in his fifties boyfriend?"

"Yes," I said. "That's the term they use. It has nothing to do with age. They are called boyfriends and girlfriends even if they are a hundred years old."

Martine told me that her English was not as good as her mother tongue, Finnish. But I had not noticed any shortcomings. Other than Finnish and English, she could also read, write and speak French, German and Russian. She had a smattering of Mandarin too, having spent a year in China as an exchange student.

After some more wandering around, we came to the last item on the agenda for the day, which was dinner. It was my suggestion. "I want to treat you to lunch or dinner at an Indian restaurant," I had told her the day before.

Martine said that she knew an Indian restaurant, but it was a little far away from where we were. So we settled for a Thai restaurant, which was right in front of us.

As we walked in, Martine told me that she purposely did not bring her car "because I knew I would be having a drink with you. Fines for even minor traffic violations are hefty here.

Cops show no mercy, especially when those violations are alcohol-related."

Though dinner was my suggestion and the main purpose behind it was to give her a good treat in appreciation of all that she had done for me, it ended up in my being given a good treat by Martine. She wouldn't let me pay. When the check came, both of us fought to grab it. I gave in when I saw customers sitting nearby watching us, amused.

"When you are in Finland, you are my guest," Martine said. "When I come to India, you can treat me to all Indian food I can eat."

After the dinner, she walked me to the door of my hostel and kissed me goodnight. She reminded me, while leaving, "Don't forget, we have a dinner date with Mom tomorrow."

6

How Swedish-Russian Rivalry Affected Finland's Destiny

July 20, 2009 – Monday

Martine came to the hostel to fetch me. She brought her car this time. As soon as she pulled in, I went to the driver's side of the car and said, "This means we won't be having any drink today. At least you won't."

"Don't be that sure," she replied. Pointing to the passenger side of the car, she added, "Get in here first."

"Another pleasant, sunny day," I said as I got into the car. "The third in a row."

"Quite a luxury in Helsinki," Martine replied.

We decided to drive around for a while before going to her mother's place for dinner.

As we passed by the harbor, Martine drew my attention to a passenger ship that was anchored there. "It will be leaving for Stockholm in a few hours," she said. Every evening a ship leaves Helsinki and reaches Stockholm the next morning. Many youngsters prefer traveling by ship to flying because it doubles as a pleasure cruise, with lots of fun onboard. "At the same time as this one leaves here, another one leaves Stockholm for Helsinki too," Martine said.

Though a working day, there were many people, mostly

women, relaxing on the beach. All the women were in two-piece swimsuits. I didn't see any of them swimming, though. Looking at them, I thought to myself, "The Helsinki sun is incapable of tanning their skin even at the height of the summer." Their skin reminded me of what Shakespeare said in *Othello, the Moor of Venice*: whiter "than snow and smooth as monumental alabaster." Not that I had a chance to feel its smoothness, though the desire was there.

When Martine was looking elsewhere, I furtively glanced at those sprawling beauties. She did catch me once, making me blush.

After some more driving around, we reached the Helsinki City Museum. The visit to the museum was quite an education for me. The exhibits, with texts explaining them, taught me a lot about Finnish history. Until then, I had only a smattering of it.

I learned to what extent Finland had suffered because of its geographical disadvantage, because of its being sandwiched between two superior rival powers of the time: Sweden to its west and Russia to its east. The two were in continual conflicts until the turn of the 19th century – i.e., until Sweden lost its supremacy in the Baltic region to Russia. Any military expedition from Russia, directed at Sweden, had to go through Finland. Apart from the geographical disadvantage, Finland's being part of the Swedish Empire also added to its sufferings at the hands of the Russians. Finland, as we said in Chapter 4, was ruled by Sweden until 1809. The sufferings were intense during the Great Northern War. The museum has a whole section dedicated to that war.

The Great Northern War

The cause of the Great Northern War (1700-1721) was Sweden's steady expansion into the coastal areas of the Baltic Sea during the 16th and 17th centuries. The expansion antagonized Russia, Denmark-Norway and Saxony-Poland. All three were looking for an opportunity to strike back at Sweden. Russia, under Czar

Peter I (later known as Peter the Great), wanted to displace Sweden as the unchallenged power in the Baltic area. The immediate goals of the other two were to regain the territories they had lost to Sweden earlier. In 1697, when Charles XII, just 14 years old, became king of Sweden, they thought that the moment they had been waiting for had arrived. They thought the Swedish power was on the decline. The three powers formed an alliance against their common enemy.

But they had underestimated the capabilities of Sweden's boy king. The war that began in February 1700 dragged on for 21 years, during which the original alliance was broken up and new ones were formed. Yes, ultimately, they achieved their goal of subduing Sweden.

By the time the war ended on August 30, 1721, Sweden had lost most of the territories it had grabbed on the southern and eastern shores of the Baltic Sea. Russia had achieved its goal: it had become the preeminent Baltic power and a major European power, displacing Sweden from that status.

The exhibits in the museum drive home to the visitors the hardships the Finns underwent during the Great Northern War. To fight the Russians in the Finnish theater, the Swedish king used mainly Finnish soldiers. Of the 60,000 Finnish soldiers in the Swedish army, only about 10,000 survived the war. There was heavy loss of lives among civilians too: the prewar Finnish population of 400,000 was reduced to about 330,000.

Ordinary Finns suffered because of the armed resistance they put up against Russian occupation. Those who did it were mainly peasants. Most of the clergy and nobility in Finland had fled to Sweden. The resistance was ruthlessly crushed and tens of thousands of Finns were captured and sent to Russia to work as slaves. The Russians also destroyed much of Finland's countryside. That was their way of denying Finland's resources to Sweden.

The Finns' hardships were more severe in the 1713-21 period, during which most of Finland was under Russian occupation and subjected to plundering and looting. The period has been recorded in Finnish history as the period of Great Wrath (*Isoviha* in Finnish). It ended with the Treaty of Nystadt (1721), which brought the Great Northern War itself to an end.

The Treaty of Nystadt, signed between Russia and Sweden, was the last of the peace treaties that Charles XII signed with his enemies in the Great Northern War. Under the treaty, the Swedish king was made to cede Estonia, Livonia, Ingria and a portion of Southeastern Finland to Russia. In fact, Russia had already occupied those territories during the war. The treaty made the occupation permanent.

It may be added that even before the treaty, Czar Peter I had begun construction of a new capital for his country in Swedish Ingria. He did it soon after he occupied it in 1703. He named the newly built city St. Petersburg and moved the capital there, from Moscow, in 1712. St. Petersburg remained Russia's capital until 1918.

Thanks to the pictures and texts displayed in the museum, I learned to what extent Finland's destiny was controlled by Sweden and Russia until the turn of the 20th century. I turned to Martine and said, "Now I know why you were not all that happy about those road signs all over the city written in Swedish and Russian."

"It is not much different from what your country went through," she said. "Call it invasion or call it colonization. It's all the same."

"You are absolutely right," I told her, with a pat on her shoulder.

"We can spend all day here," Martine said. "But you know we have things to do before the day is over."

I knew what she meant. We had to be at her mother's before it was too late. We walked back to her car.

Dinner with a Finnish Family

Martine's mother makes a decent living catering for parties. It is not a big commercial venture, and she wants to keep it that way.

Her clients are mostly her friends and acquaintances. Sometimes she prepares foods at her own house and takes them to the place where the party is held; other times she cooks at the party place itself. That she is an expert cook was evident from what she served us that night.

Pointing to the fried mushroom, she said that it was picked from the backyard of her own house and those of her friends' houses. "In Helsinki, you don't have to buy mushroom," she added. "It grows all over the place. People who have time to spare go around picking it during the season."

The tastiest item Martine's mother served was the smoked salmon. I wanted to compliment her without sounding too flattering. I put it this way: "I couldn't help recalling what my friends used to say after tasting the fish curry my mother used to make."

"What did they say?" she asked.

"That it's out of this world."

All three of them laughed. "I can't wait to taste it," the mother said.

"Plan a visit to Kerala, my home state in India, when I am there," I told her.

Her boyfriend poured me another glass of wine. I couldn't say no because it was very tasty. I didn't bother to check the brand. My admiration for Martine grew more when she successfully resisted my invitation to "taste it, at least."

"I don't want to take any chance with those cops," she kept saying.

Before leaving, I said, "Here is my offer to all three of you: Any time you come to the States or India, you have a place to stay. What I have in New York is a messy one-bedroom apartment. We can manage. But make sure that I am there when you come."

"Thank you," all three said at the same time.

"It's not a perfunctory offer," I told them. "I sincerely hope I could be your host at least once before I die."

Martine and her mother laughed. "You are not that old,"

Martine said. I gave a hug and a kiss to Martine's mother and shook hands with her boyfriend.

Martine and I walked toward her car. She took my hand when she noticed that I was too overwhelmed to speak.

While driving to the hostel, she glanced at me now and then, but decided not to disturb my silence. When we reached the front of the hostel, she got out of the car, came to the passenger's side and opened the door for me, all in silence.

She held my hand and walked me to the entrance of the hostel. Seeing me struggling to utter something and my eyes welled up, she gave me a warm embrace. "You don't have to say anything," she said. "You would do the same for me if I were in your place."

I watched her walk toward the car. She looked back before opening the door and gave me a flying kiss.

I was unable to sleep most of that night. I lay in bed, pondering over the warm hospitality I enjoyed at Martine's mother's place and the warmth and care with which Martine treated me all the three days I had been in Helsinki. "Whoever thought that a chance meeting we had in Berlin would develop into a strong bond like this one!" I said to myself. "And whoever thought that a country like Finland – where the cold season lasts as long as nine months, with no sun visible for nearly three of those months – would produce such warmhearted people like Martine and her mother!"

The experience taught me two things: One, warm friendships can develop at the most unexpected times, in the most unexpected places. Two, the character of a person has nothing to do with the climate of the country in which she is born and brought up; it is the product of her upbringing, education and mental makeup.

7

The Lesson I Learned from Three Russian Teenagers

July 21, 2009 – Tuesday

I was the only passenger on the early-morning bus that took me to Helsinki's central train station. As I approached the arch-shaped front of *Rautatieasema Järnvägsstation* – that's how the station's name was written at its entrance – I said to myself, "No, this won't be my final good-bye to Helsinki." Thanks to the wonderful time I had with my friend Martine, Helsinki has become a place I would love to go back to, again, and again.

The train to St. Petersburg had not pulled in yet. On the platform, I ran into an American couple. The first question the woman asked after we exchanged "good morning" was: "Which part of India do you come from?"

At 6:30 in the morning, in a place where Indians are a rarity, any Indian would find a question like that very cheering. "So, you have been to India, eh," I said in reply.

"Yes," the man said, "our last vacation was spent in India. It was a little over a year ago."

When I told them that I was born and brought up in Kerala, their faces lit up. "That's where we had the most enjoyable time," the woman said.

At that point, the train, with "PIETARI ST" written in front, trundled in. I was disappointed that I couldn't continue the conversation. The seats allocated to us were in separate cars.

The train left the station on time. My disappointment vanished as soon as a young Finnish woman came and sat by my side and started talking. She was a Finnish dancer, and she was going to St. Petersburg to take a one-week refresher course in Russian dance.

"Ballet?" I asked her.

"No, it has more to do with body movement than actual dancing." She used the Russian word by which that particular art form is known. I didn't get it.

As the train crossed the border between Finland and Russia, a few Russian immigration officials came and checked our passports. Another one came and took away the passports. That made me nervous. When you are in a foreign country, the one document you always want to cling to is your passport. You get nervous once it is taken away from you. Doesn't matter that the person who has taken it is an immigration official. As long he or she is out of sight, you have reason to worry. Seeing the worried look on my face, the Finnish dancer said, "You will get it back."

There was another reason for my worry: I had nothing in writing to prove that my passport was with a Russian official. A few minutes later, to my relief, a few officials returned with all the passports and started giving them back, one by one. They identified each passenger by looking at his or her face and then at the person's picture in the passport. Fortunately, I was carrying my recently-renewed passport, which had my latest picture. Had I been carrying the old passport, issued nearly 10 years before, the Russian officials would be justified in suspecting some foul play on my part. The old passport had my picture with a head full of hair. The person they were looking at was completely bald. The transformation was not gradual. It happened fast, in a two-year period.

"There could be a better way to identify the owner of the passport," I told the Finnish lady.

"Russians are known for their lengthy and rigid bureaucratic procedures," she said.

"Yes, I got a taste of it while applying for the visa to come here. The instructions and application form posted online were of no use. When I went to the Russian consulate in New York, with the application form duly filled in, meticulously following all the instructions, I was told that the form and the online instructions were outdated. They gave me a new set of forms to fill in and asked me to go back the next day. Have you been to Bangkok? The visa is stamped on arrival, with no questions asked. No wonder tourists from all over the world flock to countries like Thailand."

"I don't think things will ever be that easy in Russia," she said. Then she looked out and fell into a pensive mood. Pointing to the wooded areas the train passed through, she added, "All this was part of Finland once upon a time. The Russians grabbed it from us." She fell silent again. After a minute or so, she added, "We would rather forget all that now."

I wondered what her reaction would be to the Swedish occupation of her whole country before the Russians grabbed parts of it. On second thoughts, I decided not to open that can of worms.

Thanks to my chance meeting with her, locating the bed-and-breakfast place in St. Petersburg, where I would be staying, became easy. Her Russian friend, who had come to receive her at the central St. Petersburg train station, was familiar with the whole city and its suburbs.

As soon as my Finnish acquaintance introduced me to the Russian, I showed her the address of the place where I had to go. She told me that I had to take the metro. "We are going in the same direction," she added.

I was happy to note that she spoke good English. She helped me buy the token for the metro. While getting on the train, she said, "You have to get off at the third stop."

I was so immersed in conversation with the two ladies that I forgot to count the metro stops we passed. When the train reached the station where I had to get off, the Russian said,

"This is your stop," and pushed me toward the door. The train was crowded.

While getting off, I shouted through the din, "Come to my bed-and-breakfast place in the evening. I will treat you to the best Russian vodka."

"We'll see," they shouted back and waved good-bye to me.

Innocent Giggles and Mannerisms

Once I came out of the subway station, I was almost lost. With all the street names written only in Russian, it was impossible for me to figure out which street to take. I approached three students who were standing at the entrance to the subway and conducting some kind of survey among passengers who had just gotten off the train. The fact that they spoke no English did not stand in the way of their wanting to help me. I showed them the telephone number of the bed-and-breakfast place and indicated, using my own sign language, that I had to call that number. One of them, a smart-looking boy in a three-piece suit, readily sprang into action.

While he was busy on his cellphone, I tried to engage his two friends in conversation. Pretty girls in their teens, they didn't speak a word of English. Both of them said something in Russian and kept giggling. Though I didn't understand a word of what they said, their innocent giggles and mannerisms endeared them to me. As soon as their friend got the owner of the bed-and-breakfast place on the line, he handed me his cellphone and gestured to me to talk into it.

Before leaving New York, I had spoken with Tania, the owner, twice. A retired school teacher, she spoke fairly good English. The boy had already told her where I was standing. As soon as she heard me say "hello," she said, "You are facing Ligovsky Prospekt. Turn to your right on that avenue and keep walking. When you reach the corner of Ligovsky and Svechnoi Street, you will see a blond woman, one meter and forty-five centimeters tall, smiling at you. See you in fifteen minutes."

I didn't know how to express my gratitude to the three youngsters. I handed the cellphone back to the boy and gave him a hug. Then I put my arms around all three and held them close to me. The boy just smiled, but the girls couldn't control their giggles. "The future of Russia is safe in your hands," I told them. "Thanks a million for your help."

I knew they didn't understand anything I said, except the word "Russia," but I couldn't hold back what came straight from my heart. The girls kept on giggling and the young man said something in Russian. All three faces exuded joy.

Reluctantly, I released them from my grip and walked toward Ligovsky Prospekt, saying to myself, "Language is no barrier if people have the desire to help one another. What these three Russian teenagers have done is a reaffirmation of that basic principle in human relations."

With a heart filled with joy, and with the smiling faces of three bubbly youngsters before my mind's eye, I kept walking. I knew my destination was the intersection of two streets, where a blond woman would be smiling at me. The names of the cross-streets I was passing by didn't mean anything to me. They were all in Russian. The same was the case with the description that Tania had given of her height. Being so used to feet and inches, I was not able to readily gauge her height, which she had given in meter and centimeters.

I knew, however, that she wouldn't have any problem recognizing me. Nobody would have any problem recognizing the only Indian walking on a street in a Russian city. The moment Tania spotted me, she started beaming from ear to ear.

"This way," she said.

Illegal Operation

She led me into an old building with a rickety, wooden staircase. We walked up two flights and reached her two-bedroom apartment. When I booked the place online two months earlier, I had no way of knowing the condition of the apartment and the nature of Tania's operation. The condition of the apartment left much to be desired. But then, I couldn't have asked for more for the money I was prepared to pay. I had settled for the cheapest I found online.

In time I learned that bed-and-breakfast places like this one are many in St. Petersburg. Strictly speaking, they are illegal. But the authorities look the other way, when people with limited income supplement it in this manner.

Tania had bought her apartment from the State when the offer came after the collapse of Communist rule in the former Soviet Union. In Communist days, accommodations were given free to the needy. But even the needy had to wait for long to get them. The demand always exceeded the supply. And who got what from the State was always determined by the capacity of the claimant to grease the palm of the bureaucrat or the party official dealing with the claim. Very often, both positions were held by the same individual.

Tania let her alcoholic ex-husband continue to stay in the place after their divorce. She did it out of humanitarian consideration: "His pension was not sufficient even to buy his booze."

She occupies one of the two bedrooms and rents out the other to budget-conscious travelers like me. Her ex-husband uses the living room and sleeps on the couch. On days the extra bedroom is not rented out, she lets him use it. Once in a while, when she is financially tight, she rents out both bedrooms. On those occasions, she ships her ex-husband to her mother's place and occupies the living room couch herself. "I have to do it to make ends meet," Tania told me. "The pension that I get as a retired schoolteacher is not sufficient to maintain even the simple life I am living."

I felt happy that I was being of some help to her.

8

St. Petersburg: How a Swamp Became the Cultural Capital of Russia

July 22, 2009 – Wednesday

Until the early 18th century, there was no St. Petersburg in Russia. The uninhabited swamp on which it was built later did not even belong to Russia. It belonged to Sweden. The story of how a swamp got transformed into a modern city, and eventually the cultural capital of Russia, is also the story of Russia's transformation from an insignificant czarist kingdom to a world power.

The swamp was among the territories Czar Peter I of Russia captured from Sweden during the Great Northern War (discussed in Chapter 6). The war, which began in 1700, continued until 1721. This particular piece of land came under Russian occupation in 1703 and the czar began building a new city on it right away.

Peter I coveted this piece of land for another reason. Though marshy and uninhabited, it was strategically located. It was located at the mouth of the Neva River, where it enters the Gulf of Finland. The Gulf of Finland opens into the Baltic Sea, controlling which was part of Peter I's grandiose plan. Whoever controlled the Baltic Sea controlled the Baltic trade, a rich source of wealth in those days. The Great Northern War was fought mainly to wrest control of both the Baltic Sea and the Baltic trade away from Sweden.

To the czar, modernizing Russia meant westernizing it. To accomplish that goal, he invited the best engineers, shipbuilders, architects, craftsmen and merchants from Western Europe to come and work in Russia. He also sent hundreds of Russians to Western Europe to get the best education possible.

The city that Peter built on the Neva River delta was designed by the then-famous Swiss-Italian architect, Domenico Trezzini. He designed it in the Russian Baroque style, to which he gave a new name, the Petrine Baroque style (his way of flattering Peter) – with wide streets, huge buildings, cathedrals and palaces. Peter's ultimate goal was to build a "European paradise" and, toward that end, he channeled all the energy and resources he could muster.

Though known as a benevolent dictator, he was also very cruel at times. He ordered slaves and prisoners to work on his pet project. Even serfs were forcibly relocated from villages to the newly-acquired swamp and made to do construction work. Living and working in harsh conditions made many of the workers rebel. Those who rebelled were mercilessly executed. Sickness, starvation and executions claimed the lives of nearly 30,000 people.

In 1712, Peter moved the country's capital from Moscow to the newly-built city, which he called St. Petersburg, after his favorite patron saint. By the time the Great Northern War ended, in 1721, the czar had proclaimed himself the Emperor of Russia. That is, he wanted his kingdom to be referred to as an empire. He also insisted on being called Peter the Great.

Czar Peter I died in 1725. Even after 22 years of construction, St. Petersburg was far from "the Venice of the North" he had dreamt it to be. The honor of elevating it to that status went to the rulers who succeeded him. Designed by famed architects of the period, more palaces, cathedrals, museums and other centers of culture came up in the city.

Subsequent rulers of Russia changed the name of St. Petersburg a couple of times. When World War I broke out in 1914, with Russia pitted against Germany, the city's name was changed to Petrograd. The reason, the Russians said, was that St. Petersburg was too German-sounding.

The name was again changed after the Bolshevik takeover of the country. Vladimir Lenin, the leader of the Bolshevik-led coup of October 1917 that overthrew the Kerensky government (Nicholas II, the last czar to rule Russia, had abdicated in March) and became the head of the new government, died in 1924. In that year, to perpetuate his memory, his followers changed the city's name from Petrograd to Leningrad. Even before changing the name, the capital of the country had been moved back to Moscow. It was moved in 1918.

It may be added that the Bolsheviks were the extreme wing of the Russian Social-Democratic Workers' Party that spearheaded the Bolshevik Revolution. The party also underwent name-change a couple of times. After it came to power, it was renamed the Russian Communist Party. As Russia steadily expanded and eventually became the Union of Soviet Socialist Republics, or the Soviet Union, the Russian Communist Party became the Communist Party of the Soviet Union. By 1991, with the collapse of Communist rule and the disintegration of the Soviet Union, *Lenin* had become a name most Russians did not want to associate themselves with. In a referendum held in June of that year, the residents of Leningrad decided to restore the city's original name, St. Petersburg.

The city might have ceased to be the political capital of Russia. But it still enjoys the status as its cultural capital. It will continue to do so as long as it can preserve the historical and cultural sites dating back to Peter the Great.

The most famous site every tourist makes it a point to visit is the Winter Palace. It was the czars' official residence from 1732 to 1917 and now is part of the world-famous Hermitage Museum. I took a tour of St. Petersburg and the Hermitage Museum on July 22, 2009.

City of 42 Islands and 342 Bridges

One of the reasons why St. Petersburg is nicknamed "the Venice of the North" is that both cities consist of several islands. St. Petersburg is a collection of 42 islands linked together by 342 bridges. (This is according to a 1975 counting, our tour guide told us.) Before the first permanent bridge was built by Czar Nicholas I, in 1850, people used boats to travel from one island to another. "Nicholas I is also known as Nicholas the Unforgettable," the guide said, because of the many good things he did during his reign (1825-1855). Apart from the first bridge, he also built the first railroad – from St. Petersburg to Moscow – and built and renovated many museums.

As our tour bus entered Nevsky Prospekt (*prospekt* comes from the Dutch word *prospektiva*, meaning boulevard), one could notice that, unlike other streets in the city, it has several business establishments with names written in English. It is the city's most prominent avenue and known all over Russia. As old as St. Petersburg itself, the avenue is now the very center of the bustling city.

The tour guide named some of the beautiful buildings, bridges and landmarks the bus passed by. When we passed one of the bridges, he told us that it was called the Police Bridge, because "the chief of the St. Petersburg Police lives in that building." He pointed at a pink building at one end of the bridge.

Like most Russians I met, the guide was contemptuous of his country's Communist past. His contempt became very obvious when he described how Lenin and Stalin rose to the helm of power; and when he sarcastically referred to the erstwhile Soviet Union's much-dreaded secret police, the K.G.B. According to him, "K.G.B. stands for kindness, generosity and beauty."

Pointing to the famous cathedral in St. Petersburg, which locals call "the Church of the Saviour on the Spilt Blood" or just the "Spilt Blood Church," the guide said, "You will be surprised to know that in Soviet times, it was used as a warehouse for several years. The Communists even thought of tearing it down."

It is called the "Spilt Blood Church" because it was built on the spot where Czar Alexander II's blood was spilled, when a terrorist group, called the People's Will, attempted to assassinate him. The attempt was made on March 1, 1881, and the czar died a few days later. His son, Czar Alexander III, who ruled Russia from 1881 to 1894, built a church to preserve his father's memory. Modeled on St. Basil Cathedral in Moscow's Red Square, the Spilt Blood Church is a big tourist draw in St. Petersburg. I was disappointed that our escorted tour didn't include a visit to it.

When the guide announced that the bus was passing through the city's Red Light District, an elderly man in our group said, "Tonight, no problem."

Two girls sitting in front of him looked back and burst out laughing. "What is so funny about it?" the man asked. "I may be old, but I still have a very healthy interest in it."

St. Petersburg legalized prostitution in 1843, and it was the first city in Europe to do so.

After passing through a few more areas of the city that are of interest to tourists, we reached our main destination, the Hermitage Museum, of which the Winter Palace is the most important component.

Hermitage Museum and Winter Palace

In the beginning, the Winter Palace was only the residence of the czars. And when Czar Peter I and his family moved into it in 1708, it was an unremarkable wooden house. It was replaced in 1711 with a stone house. That too was demolished, on Empress Anna Ivanovna's orders. Anna, who ruled Russia from 1730 to 1740, commissioned Francesco Bartolomeo Rastrelli, the recently appointed court architect, to construct something that would look like a real palace. The grand palace was completed in 1735.

However, that one also was replaced several years later. Empress Elizabeth, Peter the Great's daughter who ruled Russia from 1741 to 1762, did not find the palace grand enough for her. Architect Rastrelli, on her orders, tore it down and built a new one befitting her grand vision and vanity. Unfortunately, Elizabeth was not destined to live in the new palace. She died a few months before it was completed in 1762.

It was Catherine II, known as Catherine the Great, who had the good fortune to live there. She used it as her official residence during her 34-year reign (1762-1796). Though her expansive tastes in many other areas, including sex, were questionable and subjects of gossip, those in the area of the arts won her praise from one and all. Soon after she came to power, on her husband Peter III's death (it was rumored that she had a hand in his death), she started foraying into the art world of Europe. Before she died in 1796, she had filled the palace with paintings and icons created by famous European artists.

As our tour guide led us into the green-and-white Winter Palace, which had 1,057 rooms, he gave a brief history of the place, starting with Catherine the Great's death: Though the exterior of the building has remained intact to this day, its interior was remodeled and redecorated several times. After a devastating fire in 1837 destroyed almost everything inside the palace, Czar Nicholas I, who was in power at the time, ordered that the entire interior be recreated as it was before. And he insisted that it be done in one year. Thanks to the stupendous work put in by architects Vasily Stasov and Alexander Briullov, the feat was accomplished, almost. If Catherine the Great were to visit the Winter Palace today, our guide said, she wouldn't notice any difference.

It was made part of the State-run Hermitage Museum on October 17, 1917. The State Rooms of the palace now form the most popular section of the Hermitage. It is the largest art gallery in Russia and one of the largest in the world. What started, in 1764, with 255 paintings that Catherine the Great brought from Germany, now has on display over 2.7 million artworks, created by well-known artists of different periods and representing different styles. A trivia making the rounds among art aficionados goes thus: "If you were to spend a minute looking at each exhibit on display in the Hermitage, you would need 11 years before you had seen them all."

Our guide did make it a point to take us to the most important artworks, especially the ones by world-famous artists. While in the lavishly decorated State Rooms, he made this sarcastic comment: "Now you know how the czars and czarinas lived when peasants in the country were starving."

While climbing down to the ground floor, he took advantage of another chance to delve into his country's past. Standing on the stairway's red-carpeted steps, he said: "These were the same steps that the Bolsheviks and soldiers from Kronstadt took while going up to overthrow the Kerensky government. Only the carpets have been replaced."

Standing on those steps, I thought about another notorious incident, the one that set the stage for the revolutionary change in Russia, which culminated in the October 1917 Bolshevik coup that overthrew the Kerensky government. The incident has been recorded in Russia's history as "Bloody Sunday 1905."

On Sunday, January 9, 1905, industrial workers of St. Petersburg and surrounding areas had organized a demonstration to protest against their deplorable working condition. Led by a priest by the name of Georgy Gapon, they peacefully marched on the Winter Palace, hoping to petition Czar Nicholas II on their grievances and seeking remedial action. The palace guard tried to stop the marchers at the gate. When the marchers defied and pushed ahead, the guard opened fire on them. More than 100 people were killed and several hundred injured.

The two incidents, the "Bloody Sunday 1905" and the October 1917 Bolshevik coup, changed the course of Russia's history forever.

The Hermitage Museum, we were told, gets 2.5 million visitors a year.

9

My Encounter with Russian Mafia on Busiest St. Petersburg Street

July 22, 2009 – Wednesday (Continued)

It was past 4 p.m. Our escorted tour of St. Petersburg had just ended. We were in Palace Square, outside the Winter Palace. Our tour guide gave us the option of getting back on the bus so he could take us to the point where we started the tour or of being on our own from then onward. I joined those who opted for the latter. We started wandering around Palace Square.

There were many more people, of various nationalities, hanging around the square. It was a bright, sunny day, a luxury in a city which, on average, sees only 35 sunny days a year. I decided to enjoy it to the hilt.

Palace Square is a beautifully laid-out place. The city promotes it "as an excellent example of how different architectural styles can be combined in a most elaborate and aesthetically pleasing way."

It, certainly, is aesthetically pleasing: On the northern side of the square is the beautiful, green-and-white Winter Palace, which is the central part of the Hermitage Museum. Facing the palace from the southern end is the yellow-and-white General Staff Building, which headquartered the Imperial Army General Staff in czarist days and now houses different government offices.

The building on the eastern side was formerly used by the czars' Royal Guard and now various government departments have their offices in it. And on the west is the Admiralty, Russia's naval headquarters until 1917, which now houses its naval college. The Admiralty Gardens in front of the building add to the aesthetic quality of the square.

The Alexander Column

To cap it all, there is the Alexander Column. It gets its name from Czar Alexander I, who ruled Russia from 1801 to 1825. It was built, between 1830 and 1834, as a monument to his victory over Napoleon in the 1812 war. At 155 feet and 8 inches, the Alexander Column is said to be the tallest of its kind in the world. The 600-ton column is a single piece of granite rock. Perched on top of the column is a statue of an angel holding a cross. The angel, travel brochures say, represents Czar Alexander I. There have been reports that in 1952, when the country was under Stalin's dictatorship, there was a move to replace the statue of the angel with that of Stalin. Fortunately for tourists like me, that did not happen.

The red-granite column shone brighter in the evening sun. After photographing it from various angles, I went around the pedestal of the column. The pedestal has, on its four sides, engravings and portraits that symbolize Russia's military glory. One of them shows two winged angels holding an unrolled scroll at either end. A fellow tourist translated for me the message on the scroll: "To Alexander I from a grateful Russia."

After viewing all the decorations and trying to figure out, with some help from other tourists, the messages they convey, I couldn't help wondering whether the monument *Angel de la Independencia* in Mexico City, which I had visited on April 9, 2008, was inspired by this one.

I was about to leave the Palace Square area, when a smart-looking teenager approached me. He said he was from Siberia. He did mention the name of his native town, but I didn't get it. He wanted a picture of him taken, with me by his side. "Would you mind?" he asked.

I was overjoyed. "Would this ugly man mind posing for a picture with a handsome guy like you?" I said to him, adding, "I am flattered."

He smiled and handed his camera to a passerby and showed him how to click it. I did likewise with my camera. We chatted for a couple of minutes after that. He told me that I was the first Indian he had met in his life.

"You made my day," I said and gave him a hug.

The sun had just set, and it was getting grayish. I decided to get back to my bed-and-breakfast place. I had promised Tania, the owner of the place, that I would have a drink with her before dinner.

On Nevsky Prospekt, Again

I was once again on Nevsky Prospekt, which our tour guide had talked a lot about earlier. Walking leisurely on the pavement of the most popular, fashionable street in St. Petersburg, I thought about the wonderful time I had all day. When I saw large numbers of people coming out of a movie theater, I stopped and watched.

"What could the movie be about that attracted such a big crowd?" I wondered. A couple of people in the crowd with whom I enquired proved to be of no help in satisfying my curiosity. They didn't speak English.

I was about to continue my walk when I saw five men blocking my way. All of them were smoking and looking in different directions.

"Excuse me," I said.

They pretended not to have heard me.

"Excuse me," I said again, this time loudly.

They still wouldn't move, and I was surprised.

I was about to leave the sidewalk and step onto the road so I could go around them, when I felt my right hand being caught by one of them. He said something in Russian and started pulling me toward him. I got scared. The other four were still looking away as though nothing was happening in front of them.

"Excuse me," I shouted and wriggled my hand out of the man's grip. The grip was firm.

Frightened and confused, I jumped from the sidewalk onto the road and started walking fast. After making sure that I was at a safe distance from them, I stopped and looked back. All five of them were looking at me, smirking. One of them gave me a salute. I have yet to figure out what that salute meant.

I was still nervous when I reached my bed-and-breakfast place. When Tania asked me how my day was, I said: "I have heard, and actually been warned, about the Russian mafia prowling the city. I never took it seriously – until this evening." I told her what happened.

"Yes, there are criminal gangs in the city," she said. "They are mostly after foreigners. In your case, it is very obvious that you are a foreigner." She clarified the point by touching the skin on her folded left hand with the index finger of her right hand. "I didn't want to scare you. That's the only reason why I didn't warn you about them."

"Fortunately, I was able to get out of the man's grip before they could do any damage," I told her. "I had these brochures in my left hand. When my right hand was grabbed by one of the fellows, another one could have easily reached into my pocket and emptied it. That would have been the end of my tour."

The cash I had in the pocket was not much – a few dollar and ruble bills. But it had all my credit and debit cards. Lately, with the availability of ATM machines in all important cities of the world, I have stopped carrying cash in big amounts. I have been using credit and debit cards to withdraw money in local currencies for my daily expenses. The St. Petersburg incident alerted me to the danger of putting all cards in one pocket.

That night, while in bed, I tried hard not to let this rotten incident spoil the pleasant experiences I had in St. Petersburg until then. I thought about the very first people I ran into in the city: three teenagers who went out of their way to help me. "They are the future of Russia, not these thugs," I said to myself.

In a few minutes, I was fast asleep.

10

Catherine Palace and Peterhof: WWII Damage Still Being Repaired

July 23, 2009 – Thursday

First, a confession: Until our tour guide corrected me, I was under the impression that the Catherine Palace of Pushkin got its name from the flamboyant Russian Empress Catherine II, also known as Catherine the Great. Though she did play a role in adding to its grandeur and used it as her favorite summer residence during her reign as the empress of Russia from 1762 to 1796, the palace was not built by her. Nor was it named after her. It was built by Peter the Great and named after his wife, Catherine I. Catherine I became the ruler of Russia on her husband's death in 1725. She died two years later.

Pushkin is one of the charming suburbs of St. Petersburg, about half-hour by bus from the city proper. Its original name was Czarskoye Selo, meaning the czar's village. The name change took place in 1937, in commemoration of the 100th death anniversary of the legendary Russian poet Alexander Pushkin. Pushkin, they say, is to the Russian language what Shakespeare is to the English language.

The palace that Peter the Great built was a modest one. It was rebuilt into the sprawling palace-and-park complex that we see today by his daughter, Elizabeth. Elizabeth, to repeat what we said earlier, ruled Russia from 1741 to 1762. To do the redesigning and rebuilding of the original palace, Empress Elizabeth employed her favorite architect, Francesco Bartolomeo Rastrelli, the same person who designed the Winter Palace. Additional works of expansion and embellishment were done by Catherine the Great.

What we see today, however, is a restored version of what Empress Elizabeth built and Catherine the Great embellished. The earlier one was reduced to a "charred frame" by the Nazi bombings and pillage in World War II. The restoration work began in 1957. It's quite surprising that the day we visited the place, half-century later, the work was still going on. Politics and paucity of funds halted the work several times, our tour guide told us.

We were received at the palace gate with a song by the palace orchestra. When a few couples from our group started dancing to the lovely Russian music, I whispered to a fellow tourist, "Catherine the Great would have loved to dance to this tune with one of her lovers." (Before we got off the tour bus a few minutes earlier, our guide had refreshed our memory about the empress's love life. She had many young lovers. The one she was most attached to was only 25 years old, less than half her age.) He whispered back to me, when some palace employees came around offering to sell CDs and DVDs of Russian songs and dances, "Catherine the Great's vanity wouldn't tolerate this cheap commercialism. She would have given them free."

The guide took us only through the most important rooms in the labyrinthine palace and showed us only the famous artworks displayed in those rooms. "It will take days for you to tour the whole palace," she said. Going through the luxuriously decorated private chambers, gilded ballrooms and imperial halls that czars and czarinas used – to live, work, grant audiences to subjects, and hold diplomatic receptions and gala balls – every tourist would feel that he was getting his money's worth. But he would also be reminded of the contrast between the vulgar ostentation in which the rulers of Russia lived in the capital of the country, while the vast majority lived in serfdom, many of them in poverty, in the countryside.

The Story of the Amber Room

One room that no visitor would want to miss is the famous Amber Room, whose amber panels, gold moldings, and mirrors with candles lit around them, are awe-inspiring. The story of how the Amber Room became part of the Catherine Palace is equally fascinating. It was originally part of the Charlottenburg Palace, the home of Frederick William I, the first King of Prussia. In 1716, he gave it as a gift to Peter the Great, cementing a Prussian-Russian alliance against Sweden, in the Great Northern War. The amber panels and their paraphernalia were shipped to Russia in 18 large boxes. Their first home in Russia was the Winter Palace. In 1755, Empress Elizabeth ordered the Amber Room to be moved to the Catherine Palace.

Among the thousands of art treasures the Nazis looted during World War II were the contents of the Amber Room. They justified their action, saying that the Amber Room was made by Germans, for Germans. They carted the amber panels away and recreated the Amber Room in the museum of the Königsberg Castle, on the Baltic Coast. The German territory of Königsberg was seized by the Soviet Union toward the end of World War II. Renamed Kaliningrad in 1946, it is now a Russian exclave between Poland and Lithuania. I hope to visit the castle at Kaliningrad one day, if only to get a feel of what the original Amber Room, dubbed "the Eighth Wonder of the World," looked like.

What is on display at the Catherine Palace now is a replica, created in 2003, of the original one. It could be an inadvertent omission on her part: Our guide did not mention that the stunningly beautiful Amber Room we were standing in was a replica. I wonder how many of the five million people who visit the Catherine Palace every year (the number was provided by our guide) can tell the difference, unless they have read about the fate of the original Amber Room beforehand. I couldn't, because I read about the Nazi loot and Russian repossession of it much later.

The guide did go into many other details of the Amber Room, though. One of them aroused my curiosity. While stating an obvious fact that "the candles lit around mirrors gave an illusion of space," she also mentioned the total number of candles in the room: 696. She didn't know, nor have I succeeded in finding out as yet, the significance of 696.

Our next destination was Peterhof, another gift to posterity from Peter the Great.

Peterhof: More Grandiose than Versailles?

Peterhof, meaning Peter's court, was founded in 1714. Peter the Great's original plan was to build a summer palace overlooking the Gulf of Finland. The plan he envisaged was a grand one. The palace, according to the plan, would be surrounded by a large park dotted with numerous fountains, cascades and statues. His plan became more ambitious when he visited France in 1717 and got carried away by the Versailles Palace. He decided to make Peterhof more grandiose than Versailles.

True, it did not attain that stature during his lifetime. But it did, according to some historians, once the monarchs who followed him, especially Empresses Elizabeth and Catherine II, expanded and modified it.

The Nazis, after their invasion of the Soviet Union in World War II, made Peterhof their headquarters. Once they lost the war, while retreating from Peterhof, they destroyed everything in their path. The palace and most of the *objets d'art* in the vast complex were left in ruins. Their restoration was ordered right away. But it took more than six decades' work, interrupted now and then by politicians' other priorities, for Peterhof to be brought back to the level of attraction it enjoyed in czarist days. Today, it is one of the greatest tourist attractions in St. Petersburg.

My Thirty-Day European Odyssey

By the time our tour bus reached the parking lot of Peterhof, it was 2 p.m. We had only three hours to explore whatever we fancied. "You can either follow me around or be on your own," our guide said. "The bus will leave at five p.m. sharp."

I thought it prudent to follow her. Unless you are guided, you could easily be lost in the 1,000-hectare complex, consisting of palaces; 11 parks with more than 200 fountains in them; 150 statues of Roman and Greek gods, goddesses and heroes; and so on.

The first place we visited was the main palace, also known as the Great Palace. The largest room in it is the Throne Room, magnificently decorated during the reign of Catherine the Great. The stairways leading to this room and several other staterooms are adorned with gilded statues. As we did a quick tour of the important rooms in the palace, the guide gave their names: the picture hall, the ballroom, the audience hall, the drawing room, the dining room, two Chinese study rooms, and the study that was used by Peter the Great. When the palace was reconstructed by Empress Elizabeth, she took care to restore her father's study to the exact form in which he had left it.

When we came out of the palace, we were warned to be prepared for a long walk in the park. "We'll try to cover as much as we can within the limited time we have," the guide told us.

The park has three sections: the Upper Park, the Lower Park and the Alexandria Park. The last one was Czar Nicholas I's contribution, built in memory of his wife Alexandria. The Lower Park, stretching all the way up to the Gulf of Finland, is the most attractive area. What make it so are the Great Cascade, linked to the Upper Park and its Great Palace with terraces adorned with over 40 sculptures; the Monplaisir (meaning "My [Peter the Great's] Pleasure") Palace with the Chessboard Hill; the Pyramid Fountain consisting of 505 water jets; the Orangery; the Hermitage Pavilion; the Marly Palace with the Golden Hill Cascade; and the greenery that stretches as far as the eye can see.

The most attractive waterworks in the entire complex is the Great Cascade. It was also Peter the Great's favorite cascade, we were told. It runs from the foot of the Great Palace to the Grand Canal. The canal goes all the way up to, and empties into, the Gulf of Finland. The cascade is decorated with 39 gilded bronze statues and 75 fountains. At the center of the Great Cascade is the Samson Fountain. It shows water spouting from the mouth of a lion, whose jaws are opened by Samson, the biblical hero. It is a symbolic representation of Russia's victory over Sweden in the Great Northern War. The 17 steps from the foot of the palace to the Grand Canal are decorated with gilded statues of Roman and Greek gods and heroes.

While wandering through Peterhof and enjoying the beauty of everything around, the thought did cross my mind: "If this is the outcome of Peter the Great's megalomaniacal personality and extravagant lifestyle, I don't think we should be overly critical of them."

It was close to 5 p.m. I heard the guide shout from a distance, "It's time to go."

I followed her, vowing to return to Peterhof again, and again.

11

Visit to Kazansky Cathedral; Date with Michelle; Chat with a Somali

July 23, 2009 – Thursday (Continued)

The conducted tour of the day ended in Palace Square, St. Petersburg. It was a little before 6 p.m. when the tour bus brought us there. I had another important item on the agenda for the day: a dinner date with Michelle (not her real name). It was planned well before I left New York. Michelle had called me and reconfirmed it soon after I arrived in St. Petersburg. She had named a landmark on Nevsky Prospekt as our meeting place. The time we picked for the meeting was 7 p.m., which meant that I had more than an hour to kill before meeting her. I decided to saunter down Nevsky Prospekt, enjoying its sights and sounds, again.

When I reached the Kazansky Cathedral, I saw a big crowd lounging in front of its semicircular colonnade. The Kazansky Cathedral, dedicated to Our Lady of Kazan, was built in 1801-1811. Looking at its semicircular front, one could tell that it was modeled on St. Peter's Basilica in Rome, though on a much smaller scale. Heavily damaged during the 1917 Bolshevik Revolution, it was renovated and reopened in 1932. But it was reopened not as a cathedral, but as a pro-Marxist museum: The Museum of the History of Religion and Atheism. Only in 1992, after the collapse of Communist rule in the Soviet Union, did it once again become a place of worship. It is now one of the leading Russian Orthodox churches in St. Petersburg.

I could see from outside that the church was filled with worshipers. I went in, mainly out of curiosity. The evening mass was going on. The atmosphere inside the cathedral was very spiritual, though what was going on at its two entrances was anything but. A brisk sale of candles was going on there. True, the item sold was associated with church worship, but the business activity didn't go well with the atmosphere inside.

"What was the atmosphere like during Communist times?" I asked an elderly man I ran into, after I came out of the church.

"Take a look at it," he said, pointing at the church building. "Its dilapidated condition is a testament to the Communists' attitude toward churches. It was kind of abandoned. For some time, they used it as a Marxist museum. There were hardly any worshipers. The few that came did so surreptitiously and offered prayers when nobody was watching."

He said that plans were underway to renovate the building. Admiring the crowd outside the church, he continued, "All religious people, whose religiosity had been suppressed all through the years of Communist rule, suddenly found an opportunity to open up. They are now letting loose their religiosity with great fervor."

His own faith did not suffer any suppression, he said, because he was able to escape to Paris at the height of the Communist tyranny. He came back to St. Petersburg ten years ago. "This is where I belong," he said.

Two girls were standing outside the cathedral gate, one of them holding a camera. They looked at me, smiled and said something to each other. When I smiled back, one of them asked me whether I could take a picture of them with the cathedral in the background. I was more than happy to oblige. But I did ask them a small favor in return: a picture of me, with them on either side. They jumped at the suggestion and almost squeezed me between them. The gentleman, whom I had just finished talking with, captured the scene on my camera.

After he left, I engaged the two girls in a brief conversation. They said they were from Moscow. "Are you religious?" I asked them.

So-so, the elder of the two indicated with a tilting of her right palm. She had just completed her high school and was preparing to go to college. Before deciding on what subject to major in, she wanted to learn a few languages. "Maybe English, German and French," she said. She already spoke adequate English, adequate to keep a conversation going, I mean.

The younger one had two more years to go before finishing high school. Both of them were neighbors in Moscow and had relatives in St. Petersburg. Their parents told them "to come and enjoy our summer break here."

I wished them "the very best in life," bade them good-bye and continued my walk on Nevsky Prospekt.

Stop at McDonald's

When I saw a McDonald's, I felt relieved. Not because it symbolized Western-cum-capitalist penetration of what was until recently a Communist country. Even while under Communism, St. Petersburg had been the most Westernized of all Russian cities. Going by the presence of McDonald's and other American fast-food places, it can also be called the most Americanized of all Russian cities. I felt relieved at the sight of McDonald's for another reason: I badly needed to go to the bathroom. I walked in.

Looking at the crowd inside, I thought to myself, "The fast-food chain may have problem attracting customers back in America. But not in Russia. In Russia, it not only attracts customers in droves, but those whom it does are part of the upper echelon of society."

To justify my using the bathroom, I decided to have something. I ordered a small coffee and french fries. Compared with the small coffee shops in St. Petersburg I had already visited, the McDonald's was more expensive. The customers, most of them youngsters, didn't seem to mind it. Maybe patronizing McDonald's is their way of making a statement: that they are part of the Westernized, post-Communist Russia.

Inside the toilet, I felt a little uneasy when I saw two pretty cleaning women walk in with mops and buckets. I looked around to make sure that I was not in the ladies' room. But I was the only one who felt uneasy when the women came close to our backs and did their job. They didn't care what was dangling in front of us. I finished my job and got out fast.

I had known that in Communist days, the proletariat did enjoy equal-opportunity employment. I had not known, though, that the gender equality extended to employment in toilets too. So if what I witnessed was Communism's contribution to the world, it may not be a bad thing for capitalists to emulate – especially in this day and age of growing unemployment.

I suddenly realized that I was getting late for my appointment with Michelle. I left McDonald's and walked fast toward Ekaterinsky Gardens, where she had said she would be waiting for me.

Michelle is a Frenchwoman who lives half the year in St. Petersburg and the other half in London. I first came in contact with her when my Internet search for an inexpensive place to stay in St. Petersburg took me to her website. It had a place advertised that fit my budget. Since then, I had communicated with her, through email and by phone. She was the one who guided me through the process of obtaining a tourist visa to Russia. The process was the most long-winding, and the fee the highest, of all countries I have obtained tourist visas from.

Michelle had told me that, once in St. Petersburg, I would be dealing with a woman by the name of Tania with regard to my accommodation. Only after I actually checked into Tania's place did I get an idea of the nature of the arrangement between her and Michelle. It became clearer after my meeting with Michelle.

Michelle is computer-savvy and Tania is not. In return for letting Tania use her website to advertise her bed-and-breakfast facility, Michelle gets 5 percent of the rent Tania collects from customers like me. Michelle does a few more things on the side to supplement the income from her main job, which is teaching wealthy Russians English. She conducts her class in the living room of her two-bedroom apartment. During the months she lives in London, her main income comes from offering a crash course in French, mostly to Londoners who are preparing to travel to French-speaking countries. She has a two-bedroom apartment in London too.

During the last conversation I had with Michelle before I left New York, she had asked me to keep a couple of hours of one evening free. "We'll have a drink and a quick bite," she had told me. "We'll go dutch," she had said.

"I don't mind, as long as it's an inexpensive place," I had told her.

The place she chose was a favorite haunt of foreigners living in St. Petersburg. She knew many of them by their first names. She said she picked her dates from among those foreigners because, "in St. Petersburg, men are in short supply. There are three women available for every eligible man."

Casual Attitude to Sex

"There is a bar nearby where those single women come in the evening," she continued, "ostensibly to dance, but mainly to have a good time with their picks of the evening. They are not prostitutes. They don't do it for money. They pay for their drinks. Some of them even buy drinks for their male partners. They just want to have fun. They, like me, are not willing to starve until they find the men of their dreams and settle down. Do you want to go there?"

"No, thank you," I said. "I am very happy with the date I have."

"But I am going to see another guy later," she said.

"No problem," I told her. "I meant that I am enjoying what we are doing now – having an interesting conversation over an inexpensive dinner. Let me know when it's time for you to go and meet this guy. We'll call it a night."

"I would have stayed with you longer," she said. "This guy called me yesterday. I had slept with him only once before. I felt flattered when he called and said that he wanted to see me this evening."

I haven't heard many women speak about their sex life so casually and matter-of-factly. That, too, with a stranger, at their first meeting with him.

"I like your candor," I told her.

"This is the new me," she said. "I was not like this before. I was born and brought up as a Catholic, in the south of France. The sexuality in me was so suppressed until I was nineteen. My puritan parents did a wonderful job of that. I was made to feel guilty every time I romantically thought about a guy."

"When did that epiphany occur?"

"I got married to an asshole when I was nineteen. I spent two miserable years with him. He would have made a good priest. I realized what I was missing in life only after I left my padre husband and moved to Paris. Like you, I also enjoy traveling. The more you enjoy this kind of freedom, the more difficult it becomes to settle down with one guy. But I am in no hurry. I am having a good time."

A Reformed Somali Girl

She suddenly remembered that she had to collect a book she had lent to a Somali girl who would be leaving for her country the next day. The Somali came to St. Petersburg on a scholarship to study Russian and had been living there for a year. "She is waiting for me at a café," Michelle said. "It is on the way to your bus-stop. Let's go. You will like meeting her."

I did like meeting her. She spoke with Michelle in Russian and with me in English. She spoke good English. Michelle told me that her Russian was good too. "She is more fluent than what you would expect from a person who studied it only for one year," she added.

"Are you from Mogadishu?" I asked the Somali.

"Yes, I am. But things are very hard even in the capital city. Especially for women. There is no effective central government. Until a decade ago, tribal chiefs ruled their respective turfs. Now, Al-Qaeda-type Muslim fundamentalists have taken over the areas that tribal chiefs lost control of. They want us to go back to traditional Islamic ways. And they decide what traditional Islamic ways are. I am going to miss St. Petersburg." Pointing to the glass of beer in front of her, she added, "This freedom that I am enjoying now, I won't have it when I go back."

"Will the loss of freedom extend to the way you dress also?" I asked her. I couldn't help mentioning dress because she looked very smart in the jeans and T-shirt she was wearing.

"Yes, very much," she said.

"Will they force you to get into a black tent?" I asked her.

"Black tent?" she repeated the words and burst out laughing. "That's a good description of it. I am going to use it hereafter. My friends would love to hear it. Yes, they will force me to get into that. They will also do many more stupid things. People who have not known anything else won't have any problem. It's people like me who have experienced the difference that are going to suffer."

I felt sorry for her. "I know many Muslim girls who feel the same way you do," I told her. "Try to fit in as much as you can and make life trouble-free. As long as you remain modern in your mind, your friends in the West won't have any problem with what you wear."

"I will try," she said. After taking a deep breath, she continued,

"But I am going to get out of that place at the first opportunity I get."

At that point, Michelle, who had been intently listening to our conversation, cut in to say, "I will try to help you."

"Please do it, Michelle," I said. "You will not only be saving her, you will also be saving Islam from those stupid fundamentalists. She is the future of Islam."

"I hope things work out for you the way you want," I told the Somali. "I wish you all the best."

Michelle looked at her watch, and I got the message. The message was that she was getting late for her more exciting experience of the evening.

"I have to leave for Moscow early in the morning," I said. "Thank you for the very pleasant evening."

All three of us stood up at the same time. Michelle gave me a hug and the Somali shook hands with me.

"Are you too shy to hug me?" I asked her.

She blushed. I took the liberty of kissing her on the cheek. I knew she wouldn't be in any danger because there were no mullahs around watching us. The sweet smile with which she received my kiss confirmed to me that she enjoyed it.

Pointing to the bus-stop on the opposite side of the street, Michelle said, "That's where you get your bus. I know you had a long day today. May be too tired to walk. Better to take a bus."

It was only a few yards from where we were that the Russian mafia had attempted to mug me the day before. The pleasant note on which this day ended cleansed my mind of that bitter experience.

12

How Three Russian Ladies Made My Journey to Moscow Pleasant and Easy

July 24, 2009 – Friday

The St. Petersburg airport is a good two-hour ride by train and bus from the city proper. The travel agent, through whom I had made my hotel reservation in Moscow, had told me that the cheapest way to get to the airport was a train-cum-bus combination. I was on my way to the airport, en route to Moscow.

I had also been advised by the same travel agent about where in St. Petersburg to catch the metro; where to change trains; and where to catch the connecting bus to the airport. But I had misheard the name of the station where I had to switch trains as Moscow Square.

"There is no station called Moscow Square," a young lady on the train, whom I requested to alert me when we arrived there, said. "It's Moskovskaya. I will be changing trains at the same place. You can come with me."

"You are my savior," I told her. "Even if there is a station called Moscow Square, I wouldn't have recognized it. If you don't know Russian, you are lost here. Nothing is written in any language other than Russian. You know that is not the case in other major European cities. Even in China English is becoming very popular."

"Don't worry," she said. "We are getting there. It won't be as fast as some of us want it. But we certainly are opening up."

"You speak very good English. Where did you learn it?" I asked her.

"In London," she said. "I teach English and French at the university here."

"Wow, I am happy for you," I told her. "Are there many students keen on learning foreign languages?"

"Yes, my English class is always full. We always have more students wanting to enroll than we can accommodate. Many of them have to be put on the waiting list for the next session"

"I am glad to hear that people are recognizing the importance of learning English," I said. "You will agree with me that in this era of information technology, progress is not possible without some knowledge of English. Why is it that even in a cosmopolitan city like St. Petersburg, announcements on trains and buses are only in Russian?"

"I told you we'll get there. Give us some time."

I could sense that she didn't like my question. What she said next confirmed it: "Some of the Indians I come across here are horrible in their use of English. How do you explain that?"

The question made me a little uneasy. After a few seconds, I was able to come up with an explanation: "I am sure you are talking about the Indian students you meet at your university. Most students who are good at English prefer going to American and British universities. Maybe the students whom you are talking about are science and technology students. Or those who came here to learn the Russian language. English is not their forte."

"You may be right," she said, more to change the topic than in agreement with what I said.

"This is Moscow Square," she said when the train slowed down and the next stop was announced.

"No," I told her. "Moskovskaya. Learn to say it properly."

She liked the way I handled her teasing. Both of us laughed and got off the train. I followed her to another platform and got on the train that arrived there. "I will be going further," she said. "I will show you where you have to get off to catch the airport bus."

We were together for 15 more minutes and talked about many more things. I couldn't help bringing up last year's presidential election in Russia which was mocked in the U.S. media. In terms of the constitution of the Russian Federation, one could serve as president only for two consecutive terms. Vladimir Putin's two terms ended in 2008. In the next election, held in March 2008, his hand-picked nominee, Dimitry Medvedev, won the presidency by a landslide. Within hours of taking office, on May 7, 2008, Medvedev nominated Putin as prime minister of the country and the Russian Parliament confirmed it the next day. Rumors were rife at the time that the whole thing was engineered by Putin with a view to clinging to power after his constitutionally mandated two terms ended. He was the real power behind the Medvedev presidency, the Western media reported.

"Why is Putin reluctant to give up power completely?" I asked her.

"Many of us feel the same way," she said. "But then, unless you are really into politics, these things don't bother you much. I am not political. Where have you been staying in St. Petersburg?"

I could tell that she was more interested in changing the subject than getting an answer to her question. My answer to her next question touched upon another topic most Russians are uncomfortable talking about: alcoholism. When she asked me whether I enjoyed my stay at the bed-and-breakfast place, I replied, "Yes, except for the constant grunting and frequent use of the bathroom by the hostess's alcoholic ex-husband. He and I had to use the same bathroom." I told her about the post-divorce modus vivendi between the hostess and her ex-husband.

"Yes," she said, nodding her head, "alcoholism is a big problem in our country."

When the train arrived at the station where I had to get off, she shook hands with me and said, "I enjoyed talking with you."

"I am so happy," I replied, holding her hand between my palms, "that my trip to Moscow started this pleasantly."

She blushed. The pretty university teacher looked prettier when she blushed.

She Promotes Russia Abroad

An equally pleasant experience was waiting for me on my flight by Aeroflot to Moscow. Sitting next to me on the plane was another attractive Russian woman. She also spoke good English. She had been living in Stockholm for five years and was going to Moscow on a two-week vacation. Her parents and many childhood friends still lived in Moscow, she told me. Her boyfriend, a farmer, lived in the northern countryside of France. She visited him as often as her work schedule permitted. She worked in corporate communications. Her main job was making PowerPoint presentations to Swedes and other Scandinavians on business opportunities available in Russia and on how to go about setting up businesses there. She was one of the beneficiaries of Russia's latter-day opening up to the world.

"We may not become as open as America," she said. "But there is no going back on the openness you are witnessing now. The same is true of the slow process of democracy that you can see evolving now. We have a long way to go. There is no doubt about it."

I showed her the address of the hotel in Moscow where I would be staying and asked how to get there from the airport. She explained to me the quickest and cheapest way of doing it. Then she opened her handbag and took out a map of the Moscow metro system, which had everything written in Russian.

Pointing to a spot on the map, she said, "This is Partizanskaya metro station. It was called Izmailovsky Park before. This is where you will be getting off. Your hotel is only walking distance from here." Pointing to another spot on the map, she added, "I am going in the same direction up to this place. I will show you which train to take from there."

After getting off the plane, we got on an airport shuttle bus, which took us to a nearby train station. The train to Moscow City was about to leave. We had to buy tickets in a hurry and run to catch it. "This airport-to-Moscow express train service was recently introduced," she told me as we ran to the train.

Once we reached the crowded Moscow station, she started walking fast and gestured to me to follow her. Maybe she was getting late for her connecting train. I followed her like an obedient child, though I am old enough to be her father, when she switched from platform to platform and train to train. When we reached the station where we had to switch to different trains, she gave me the only railway map she had and said, "I will pick up another one on my way." She told me the number of stations I would be passing before reaching Partizanskaya. She knew that for this illiterate in the Russian language, the number of stations I would pass was the key, not their names.

I could see that she was in a hurry. But I couldn't let her go that fast when she shook hands with me. I kept holding her hand and said, "I don't know how to thank you. Without your help, I would have been lost. How much time I would have wasted, and how much frustration I would have gone through trying to figure out all this by myself."

"Don't worry," she said, "it's my duty. Take the first train that arrives on this platform. All of them go in the direction of your hotel."

She gave me a hug and rushed onto the train that arrived on the opposite platform. I was overwhelmed by the touchingly helpful nature of the young lady, who was a total stranger until three hours before. The train I had to take arrived in a minute or so.

The Partizanskaya station is on the outskirts of Moscow. Compared with the few stations in Moscow I had just gone through, it is a simple one. I knew it was only a few minutes' walk from the station to Izmailovo Hotel. Getting there was made easier by another young Russian woman. We got off the same subway car. I asked her which exit was closer to the Ismailovo Hotel.

"I am going to the same hotel," she said. Then she took a good look at me and added, "Are you from India?"

When I told her yes, she gave me a big smile.

"I thought so," she said. "I lived in Vizag for a year. I know you call it Visakhapatnam. I loved my stay in India."

She worked for Gazprom, the largest natural gas company in Russia, and one of the largest in the world. She was part of a Russian team that was sent to Visakhapatnam, in the southern Indian state of Andhra Pradesh, when Gazprom had entered into a collaborative venture with India's Oil and Natural Gas Corporation. Based in Siberia, where Gazprom's main operations are, she had come to Moscow to attend a conference. The conference was held at Izmailovo Hotel.

The hotel is a sprawling complex with four wings – Alfa, Beta, Vega, Gamma-Delta – each functioning as a separate entity. Built on the eve of the 1980 Moscow Olympics, the entire complex has 7,500 rooms and can accommodate 10,000 guests at a time. I was booked in the Vega wing of the hotel. The India-loving Russian showed me the direction in which I should be going and shook hands with me. She was staying in the Gamma-Delta wing.

"I will be staying here for three days," I told her. "We may run into each other again."

I was pleasantly surprised to know, when I checked into the hotel, that the TV in my room had access to the BBC News in English, 24 hours. A small consolation, given the fact that the rent I was paying was beyond my budget. Some miscommunication between me and the agency that made the hotel reservation for me caused me to pay more than what I was told originally.

After relaxing for a while in my room, I came out and wandered around the sprawling hotel complex. Toward sunset, I walked into one of the restaurants in the complex. I sat in an isolated corner of the restaurant and ordered a beer.

A two-piece band, consisting of a keyboard and a guitar, was playing at the time. The keyboardist and the guitarist took turns in singing. The former sang Russian songs and the latter English. What made my first evening in Moscow memorable was not the restaurant or the band or the singing. It was something else.

Whenever the keyboardist sang classical Russian songs, a young girl, maybe eight or nine years old, rose from her seat and started dancing. She did not do it in the dance area in front of the musicians. She did it in the narrow space between tables. The parents of the girl and all the patrons in the restaurant enjoyed the dance. The girl was not at all self-conscious. One could tell that she enjoyed dancing more than we enjoyed watching it. The parents allowed me to take a picture of their daughter's dance. I told them that she was so talented and, if nurtured properly, would become a great dancer.

I couldn't tell whether they understood what I said. But they knew that what I said was something good. Their appreciative smile and nod in response to what I said confirmed to me at least that much. Hardly anyone around there spoke any English. Not even the waiters.

Russians Dance to "Lady in Red"

The ignorance of English didn't stand in the way, though, of their enjoying all the English songs the guitarist sang. Three couples danced to most of those songs. But when the guitarist sang "Lady in Red," the small dancing area became crowded.

The romantic song, by Chris de Burgh, has been a favorite of mine ever since I first heard it. The album with the song on it, when released in 1986, had instantly become a best-seller in 25 countries. But I couldn't figure out why a small crowd in an unremarkable restaurant in Moscow found this particular song their favorite of the evening. "Are they still getting nostalgic when they hear the word red?" I wondered.

13

Tour of Kremlin and Red Square; a Crash Course in Moscow's History

July 25, 2009 – Saturday

It was my first full day in Moscow. I was determined to utilize every minute of it. I enquired at the hotel's information desk whether there was any guided tour that I could take to see Moscow.

"Yes, there is one leaving at 10 a.m.," the lady at the desk said. "It's a small group. You will be going around on a mini-bus. The tour guide is very knowledgeable. You will love it. Would you like to join?" I said yes.

"Enjoy the tour," she said and handed me the ticket.

Sitting next to me on the tour bus was a geologist from a Siberian town. She did tell me the name of the town, but I had never heard it before. She was also staying at Izmailovo Hotel, but in a different wing from mine. Like the other Siberian who guided me from the metro station to the hotel the day before yesterday, she too came to Moscow to attend a job-related conference. She was pretty, elegantly dressed and spoke English. She may be in her late 20's or early 30's. The thought that I was going to be sitting next to her throughout the tour made me happy.

As soon as our tour guide came on the bus, she announced

that the highlights of the tour would be visits to the Kremlin and Red Square. There is hardly any tour of Moscow that doesn't include these two places. Both are parts of the same complex separated by one of the walls of the Kremlin. In 1990, the UNESCO added the complex to its list of the World Heritage Sites.

As the bus left the hotel, the guide started her commentary. She started it with a brief history of Moscow. The geologist from Siberia whispered to me that she had a chat with the guide earlier. She was a history teacher at a local school, doing this job on weekends to supplement her income. "Moscow," the guide said, "is the most populous European city today and the fifth-largest city in the world." Its present population is about 12 million.

The name of the city and of the river that runs through it is *Moskva*, in the Russian language. Historians have traced the origins of the word *Moskva* to the language used by some Finno-Ugric tribes who were the first to settle in the territory that we now call Moscow. The word has been variously translated. Two widely accepted translations are "marshy place" and "mossy plain." It was on the marshy land at the confluence of the Neglina and Moscow Rivers that the city was founded, in 1147.

The man credited with the founding was Yuri Dolgoruky (Yuri the Long-Armed), the Grand Duke of Kiev. A wooden fort that he built on the marshy land, together with a few wooden structures that came up inside and around it, constituted the Moscow Kremlin in its incipient stage. The word "Kremlin" is derived from the Russian word *kreml*, which means fortress or citadel.

Though the city that grew around the Kremlin was destroyed by the Tatars (a Mongolian sect) in 1208, it was rebuilt and rapidly expanded soon thereafter. Attack and destruction of the city by the Mongols occurred a few more times, but the residents repulsed the attacks and rebuilt their city every time. In the late 13th century, it became the capital of the Grand Principality of Muscovy. The residents of Muscovy came to be called Muscovites. Since 1326, Moscow has also been the spiritual center of the Russian Orthodox Church. Until then, that status had been enjoyed by another Russian principality, Vladimir.

In the early 19th century, Moscow again needed rebuilding. Napoleon Bonaparte invaded Russia in 1812. By the time he and his *Grande Armée* reached Moscow, on September 14, the residents of the city had evacuated, but only after setting most of it on fire. The scorched-earth policy, deliberately followed by the Russians, left Napoleon and his troops with nothing to live on. All supply lines had been destroyed. A humiliated Napoleon led his surviving troops out of Moscow on October 19. Muscovites started rebuilding it soon after their victory over the French.

With the Kremlin as its center, Moscow expanded outward in concentric rings, each ring representing a particular stage in the city's development. One can get some idea of what the city was like at each stage of its development from some of the buildings that are still extant on the ring roads – the Boulevard Ring, the Garden Ring, the Moscow Ring Road, etc. – and the radial roads from the Kremlin that connect the ring roads.

Izmailovo Hotel is situated on the periphery of the city, beyond the Moscow Ring Road. As we drove toward the Kremlin, we passed by mansions, most of which the guide told us were owned by Moscow's new billionaires. The city now has the largest number of billionaires in any city anywhere in the world. They live in their luxury apartments in the city on weekdays and spend their weekends in their mansions in the suburbs or dachas in the countryside.

As we entered a ring road or radial road, the guide told us its name. As we passed by certain types of buildings, she mentioned which period they represented. Pointing at the four- and five-story apartment buildings we were passing by, she said that they were built during the Khrushchev era.

Nikita Khrushchev, as secretary of the Communist Party of the Soviet Union, was at the helm of power from 1953 to 1964. He built those apartments when Moscow was faced with acute housing shortage, caused by the sudden influx of working class people from the countryside. Most workers and low-paid white-collar employees were allowed to live in those apartments rent-free. Their children and grandchildren now own those apartments thanks to the restructuring of the economy (*perestroika*), introduced by Mikhail Gorbachev in the mid-1980s.

Stalin's "Seven Sisters"

We next entered the ring that represents the previous phase in the city's development. It's known as the Stalinist phase. Josef Stalin, the guide reminded us, was the dictator of the Soviet Union from 1928 to 1953. Pointing at the Hotel Ukraina on the other side of the Moscow River, she said that it was one of Stalin's "Seven Sisters." She also briefly narrated the story behind the "Seven Sisters."

In 1947, Moscow celebrated the 800th anniversary of its founding. To commemorate the event, Stalin ordered that eight skyscrapers, of the type that existed only in major cities of Europe and the United States at the time, be built in different parts of Moscow. Structures of 30-to-35 stories were considered skyscrapers in those days. By building such structures, Stalin was trying to prove to the West that "We Can," which, by the way, was the architectural slogan he popularized around that time. Only seven skyscrapers were completed in his lifetime, and hence the nickname "Seven Sisters." The nickname was also an allusion to the monotony of their style – terraced or tiered – mockingly referred to as "wedding-cake" style.

While Stalin was trying to rival the West in building skyscrapers, millions of his countrymen were starving and living in cramped communal apartments. His justification was that he built them without spending a penny on labor. He used thousands of men and women languishing in the Gulag and German prisoners of war captured during World War II to do the job.

Though there was a serious housing shortage in Moscow

at that time, only two of the "Seven Sisters" were used for residential purpose. Of the rest, two were turned into hotels – Hotel Ukraina and Hotel Leningradskaya; two were used as government offices, including the offices of the Ministry of Foreign Affairs; and one became the main campus of the Moscow State University. The last one, built on the Sparrow Hills, is the most impressive of all. Pointing at it, the guide said that it was only one of the nearly 1,000 buildings, spread all over the city, in which the Moscow State University functioned. She also gave us some interesting pieces of information about this prestigious university.

It was founded in 1755 by the famous Russian polymath Mikhail Lomonosov. Its original name was the Imperial Moscow University. In 1940, the name was changed to the Lomonosov Moscow State University, in honor of its founder. The university's motto: "Science is the clear learning of truth and enlightenment of the mind." It now has 40,000 students, 4,000 of them foreigners; 6,000 faculty members; and 5,000 researchers. Its library has nine million books, two million of them in foreign languages. The guide also named some of the MSU alumni who distinguished themselves in politics, science and literature. A few of them were Nobel laureates.

In a few more minutes, we were in front of the Kremlin. It is enclosed by three walls that form an irregular triangle. The 2205-meter-long walls, varying in height from five to 19 meters, have 20 towers. They were built by Italian architects, commissioned by Ivan III, in the last decade of the 15th century. The reign of Ivan III, also known as Ivan the Great, lasted from 1462 to 1505.

Some of the towers have gates underneath. The only gate the public is allowed to use now is the one under the Kutafya Tower. As we went in, the guide said that the most beautiful of the Kremlin towers was the Spasskaya (Savior) Tower. There are many legends and miracles associated with that tower. That could be the reason why, the guide said, until a few years ago, all visitors to the Kremlin had used the gate underneath the

Spasskaya Tower. The traffic through that gate became heavier and heavier and, by 1999, it became so uncontrollable that the authorities ordered it closed. Talks are now going on to reopen it.

Indeed, the 71-meter-tall Spasskaya Tower, with a huge clock and belfry on top, and a ruby-red star shining above them, is beautiful. The tower was built in 1491 by the Italian architect Pietro Solario. The belfry and clock were added later. The red star was mounted in 1937, by Soviet authorities, replacing the replica of the double-headed Russian eagle that had been there until then. The clock chimes every quarter hour, and the chime is broadcast by radio to the entire nation, announcing the Moscow time. Russia as a whole has 11 time zones.

Cathedral Square

Once we passed through the Kutafya Tower gate, we were taken straight to the centrally located Cathedral Square. Pointing at the churches around, the guide told us that after the 1917 Bolshevik takeover of the country, they had ceased to be places of worship. They were reopened to the public in 1990, some as museums. The guide took us to three of them, saying that they were "superb examples of Russian church architecture at its height in the late 15th and early 16th centuries."

The Cathedral of the Assumption, built in 1475-79 in the Italian-Byzantine style, with elegant arches and five golden domes, is the oldest. The coronation of the first Russian czar, Ivan IV (the Terrible), took place in this cathedral, in 1547. According to a popular Russian gossip, during World War II, when the invading Nazis reached Moscow in the winter of 1941, Stalin secretly ordered for a special service to be held in this church to pray for the country's liberation.

Another one-time place of worship, which is now a museum, is the Cathedral of the Annunciation. The original structure, built in 1484-89, was destroyed in a fire in 1547. It was rebuilt in 1562-64. It has a cluster of chapels with golden roofs and domes. Inside he cathedral are a number of early 15th-century icons created by "the greatest of all Russian icon painters," Theophanes the Greek and Andrey Rublyov. The icons are a big tourist draw.

The third cathedral we visited, the one dedicated to St. Michael the Archangel, has a special place in Russia's history. It contains the tombs of all the rulers, except one, of Muscovy and Russia, from the 14th century until Peter I came to power, in 1682. In 1712, Peter I moved the country's capital from Moscow to the newly-built St. Petersburg. One of the greatest treasures of this place is the burial chamber of Ivan the Terrible. Being the first Russian ruler to take the title czar, he wanted to make his burial chamber very special and he oversaw its construction himself. The Cathedral of St. Michael the Archangel, too, is functioning as a museum now.

The Broken Czar Bell

Another great tourist attraction in the Kremlin is the Ivan the Great Bell Tower. When built in 1508, this 81-meter-tall structure was also used as a watchtower. Until the 19th century, no building in Moscow was allowed to be taller than this. At the foot of the tower sits the 210-ton Czar Bell, cast in 1733-35. The bell never rang, because it broke soon after it was cast. In 1737, a huge fire had swept through Moscow and engulfed the Kremlin. The water used to extinguish the fire fell on the Czar Bell that had just been cast and broke it. The 11.5-ton broken piece is still lying near the rest of the bell.

Another item that sits near the Czar Bell is the Czar Cannon, cast in 1586. And next to the cannon are the Cathedral of the Twelve Apostles and the Patriarchal Palace. The cathedral was the patriarch's private chapel. The cathedral-cum-palace was built in the mid-17th century on the initiative of Patriarch Nikon. His tenure as head of the Russian Orthodox Church, from 1652 to 1658, was marked by frequent feuds with Czar Aleksei. The patriarch wanted his residence to rival that of the czar, the Terem

Palace, in grandeur. The cathedral, like other places of worship in the Kremlin, was closed in 1918, in the wake of the Bolshevik Revolution. The whole building is now part of the Great Kremlin Palace complex, not open to the public.

The Great Kremlin Palace was built in 1838-49 as a royal residence. The guide showed us from a distance a few other structures, already in existence since long before, that were made parts of the palace complex. The Terem Palace, one of them, was the official residence of the czar until the Bolshevik takeover of the country. Another one is the Palace of Facets. It is called so, the guide said, because of its "exterior finish of faceted, white stone squares." Built in 1487-91 by Italian architects, it was used by the czars as a banquet and reception hall. The Great Kremlin Palace also incorporates several old churches, dating from 1393.

It is connected to the Armory Palace, built in 1844-51, which now houses the Armory Museum. The museum has a large collection of the czars' treasures. We saw only two buildings within the Kremlin that were built in the Soviet era: the School for Red Commanders, built in 1932-34; and the Palace of Congresses, built in 1960-61. Needless to say, it was the structures and monuments built by the czars and rulers before them that we found awe-inspiring.

Red Square

By the time we came out of the Kremlin and entered Red Square, it was 4:30 p.m. The guide gave us a brief history of the square. First she cleared the misunderstanding that many people have – I am one of them – about the word 'Red' in 'Red Square.' "It has nothing to do with communism or the Communist Party's association with red color," she said. "Nor does it have anything to do with the red color of most of the buildings around or of the Kremlin walls," she added. Russians call the place *Krasnaya Ploschad*. *Krasnaya* is derived from *krasnyi*, which in Old Russian meant beautiful. In fact, in the beginning,

Red Square was known as Trinity Square, after Trinity Cathedral that stood on its southern end. Only from the mid-17th century did Russians begin to call it *Krasnaya Ploschad,* meaning the beautiful square. *Krasnaya* means red only in contemporary Russian.

In the beginning, again, Red Square was a shanty town of wooden huts that housed a bunch of peddlers, criminals and drunks. It was cleaned up toward the end of the 15th century, on orders from Ivan III. Since then, it "has been the scene of executions, demonstrations, riots, parades and speeches," the guide said. Two annual parades held here in Soviet times – the Labor Day Parade on May 1 and the Victory Day Parade on May 9 – were known for their pomp and pageantry. (It was on May 9, 1945 that Nazi Germany surrendered to the Soviet Union, thus ending World War II in the Western sector.) The Soviet authorities used the occasions to show off their military might to the rest of the world.

The tradition stopped with the disintegration of the Soviet Union in 1991. "Talks are underway to revive the annual parades," the guide said. Lately, the 800,000-square-foot area of Red Square has been used for rock concerts, classical music performances, fashion shows, and various festivals. Moscow ushered in the third millennium with a huge firework display and street party in Red Square.

A few other structures that came up around the square over centuries, since Ivan the Great cleaned it, added to its attraction and importance. The most beautiful of them is the Cathedral of St. Basil the Blessed. It was built in 1554-60 by Ivan the Terrible to commemorate his victory over the Tatars of Kazan and Astrakhan. Legend has it that, soon after it was built, the Italian architect who designed it was blinded by the Russians. They did it to prevent him from replicating the beautiful cathedral elsewhere.

Pointing to the white stone platform near the cathedral, the guide said that it was used in czarist days for proclaiming royal

My Thirty-Day European Odyssey

decrees and edicts to the masses. Once a year, the czar would also stand on the platform and give audience to his subjects.

The State Historical Museum, built in 1875-83, is on the opposite end of the square from St. Basil. The museum has millions of objects that focus on Russian history and culture. Adjacent to it, at right angle, is the sprawling, arcaded building that houses the famous department store, GUM. GUM is acronym for *Glavnyi Universalnyi Magazin* in Russian, meaning the main universal store. Built in 1889-93, it was state-owned in Soviet times. Those were the days when almost every consumer item, including bread, was in short supply. People, we were told, used to line up in front of GUM as soon as fresh supplies arrived. Sometimes the line would extend all the way to the end of Red Square. Since its privatization in 1993, GUM has been selling mostly high-priced fashion goods, most of them imported, which average Russians cannot afford.

Facing GUM from the opposite side of the square is the Lenin Mausoleum, inside which his embalmed body still lies. I was disappointed to hear that the mausoleum was closed for the day. It is open from 10 a.m. to 1 p.m. every day, except on holidays, Mondays and Fridays.

We were now at the center of Red Square. "This brings us to the finale of the tour," the guide said. "You are free to wander around during the remaining few minutes. The bus will leave at 5:30 p.m."

Lenin Mausoleum

Which meant that we had a little over 30 minutes to do whatever we felt like doing. "A visit to the Lenin Mausoleum was very much on my agenda when I planned my Moscow trip," I told my Siberian fellow tourist. "I don't know when I am going to be here next. Let me go and see as much of the mausoleum as I can from outside. Would you like to come?"

"Yes, let's go," she said.

The Lenin Mausoleum is small, but attractive. Built in layers of red, gray and black granite, it snugs the Kremlin wall and blends well with it. It was completed in 1930, replacing the wooden mausoleum that had already been built there after Lenin's death in 1924. These days, it doesn't attract as many tourists as it used to in Communist times. In fact, Russians are less interested in visiting it than foreigners. The following conversation I had with the lady from Siberia should give an idea of what the present generation of Russians thinks about Lenin – and other Communist leaders, dead or alive, for that matter.

Pointing to the closed mausoleum, she whispered to me that what was lying inside was not Lenin's embalmed body, but his look-alike in wax. "His actual body was shipped away long ago and buried elsewhere," she said, and followed it with a chuckle.

The chuckle made it clear that I was not supposed to take what she said seriously. I wouldn't have, even without the chuckle. I had heard another story about what nearly happened to Lenin's body. I told her that.

In 1991, then-Russian President Boris Yeltsin had suggested removing the body from the mausoleum and burying it next to the tomb of his mother, Maria Alexandrovna Ulyanova, at the Volkov Cemetery in St. Petersburg. Yeltsin's successor, Vladimir Putin, brushed aside the idea, arguing that it would be an insult to all those people who visited the mausoleum over the years, mainly to pay their respects to Lenin. "I know Putin himself cares two hoots for Lenin and his legacy," I added. I also followed it with a chuckle.

"You are right," she said, "I mean the last part, that Putin doesn't care much for Lenin."

At that point, we heard our guide shout from a distance: "It's time to go. The bus will be leaving in two minutes."

14

Lovers and Newlyweds in Moscow Seal Their Bond with Padlocks

July 26, 2009 – Sunday

The tour I took the day before was educative and interesting. But it was also very tiring. I slept like a log all through the night. By the time I got up in the morning, it was well past 9 o'clock.

I had nothing specific planned for this day. So I decided to wander around the city on my own, at my own leisurely pace. I remembered what our guide had told us: the underground metro was always preferable to surface transportation. Being a Sunday, it would be totally hassle-free, I thought to myself.

In Moscow, getting from one place to another by road can often be a nightmarish experience. The city's population has been growing rapidly and public transportation has not been able to cope with that growth. Traffic jams are so frequent that it can sometimes take three hours for people to get to work. There are no yellow cabs or government-regulated taxi system in Moscow. There are private cars illegally operating as taxis. "Be careful," the guide had warned us, "if you speak English, the fare will go up." The authorities have started cracking down on this illegal operation.

Three-fourths of Moscow's 12 million residents rely on the underground metro to get around the city. The metro system, started in 1935, is well maintained and runs efficiently. Some of the 188 underground stations were also built as bomb-shelters. That explains why they are deep below the surface. Only in Stockholm and Oslo have I seen subway train tunnels built as far below the surface as in Moscow. In the Scandinavian cities, however, they were built that far below not with a view to sheltering people from bombs, but to enabling huge ocean liners to pass freely above them.

Some Moscow metro stations are as labyrinthine and confusing as the one in Times Square, in New York City, especially for a newly-arrived person. Built about eight decades ago, most of them have no escalators or elevators, except at the entrance and exit. But there are redeeming features in many of them: With "elaborate architecture, marble decoration, stained glass, statuary, and chandeliers," some stations look like "art galleries," according to the travel brochures I browsed. I left my hotel room in the morning, hoping to give myself the pleasure of visiting some of those "galleries."

"What a difference two days make!" That was the first thought that crossed my mind, as I arrived at the Partizanskaya station. There were only a few passengers on the platform. When I arrived at this station two days before, it was teeming with men and women jostling with one another to get on or off the train. "But then," I reminded myself, "unlike today, a Sunday, the day I landed here was a working day." In any case, I started enjoying the slow pace of the day. The train arrived in a couple of minutes.

The first place I wanted to visit was the Tretyakov Gallery. I got off at the Tetryakovskaya station, from where it's only walking distance to the gallery.

Visit to Tretyakov Gallery

The State Tretyakov Gallery is one of the largest in Russia. It started as a private collection of the well-known Moscow industrialist and philanthropist, Pavel Mikhailovich Tretyakov (1832-1898). It was named after him later.

Tretyakov opened his private gallery to the public in 1870. And, in 1892, he donated his entire collection to the City of Moscow. After the Communist takeover of the country, "art was bought, donated, or 'transferred', from other museums, private collections, cathedrals and monasteries." Naturally, the collection at the Tretyakov Gallery grew rapidly. It now houses over 130,000 works of art – icons, paintings, graphics and sculptures. They represent the evolution of Russian art over 10 centuries – from the 11th to the 20th. Under the Nationalization Decree signed by Lenin in 1918, it became the State Tretyakov Gallery.

I could have spent all day at the gallery, and still would have glanced only a small part of its collection. There was a lot more of Moscow that I had yet to explore. So, after spending about two hours at the gallery, I came out. The next place on my itinerary, which I had marked on the tourist map I was carrying, was Bolotnaya Square. It was close to where I was.

A "Weird" Moscow Custom

At the time I arrived, the place was crowded with newly-wed couples and their friends and relatives. Many of them looked as though they had just come out of the wedding ceremony. It has become a custom among some of the newlyweds in Moscow to come to Bolotnaya Square and get photographed in their wedding dress.

The nearby Luzhkov Bridge is known for another "weird Moscow custom" – the custom of lovers and newlyweds sealing their bond by hanging padlocks on metal trees placed on the bridge and then throwing the key into the canal below. The canal that flows into the Moscow River separates Bolotnaya Square from Bolotniy Garden.

Throwing the key away symbolizes the permanence of the union. If either of the couple wishes to end the union, he or she will have to dive into the bottom of the canal to retrieve the key from among the thousands that are lying there. According to a joke making the rounds in Moscow, since the practice began, the divorce rate in the city has gone down considerably. The reason? Many married couples prefer staying married to going through the impossible task of retrieving the key from the cold, polluted waters of the canal.

The practice, it is said, had its origins in an ancient Russian custom. According to a Russian lore (Russians are fond of folklore), young married couples used to be locked inside a granary shed on their wedding night. The purpose behind it was to provide them some privacy, away from the wedding-day crowd. A few years ago, some romantic Muscovites decided to adapt the ancient custom to modern times. The newlyweds' hanging "Padlocks of Love," as they call those locks, on "Trees of Love" placed on the Luzhkov Bridge is the outcome of that adaptation. The practice caught on so fast that, in a couple of years, the bridge was packed with metal trees and additional ones had to be placed on the street next to the bridge. It spread still further. Today, one of the travel brochures says, there are 10 streets in Moscow where newly-bonded couples can go and demonstrate their inseparability by placing padlocks on metal trees.

As I walked on the for-pedestrians-only Luzhkov Bridge, I was amused by another spectacle: grooms cradling their brides and carrying them from one end of the bridge to the other. After enjoying the scene for a while, I crossed over to the other side of the bridge and walked into the vast Bolotniy Garden.

Bolotniy Garden

Everything was quiet around the Bolotniy Garden. The quietude was a welcome change from the noisy scenes of Bolotnaya Square. I was aware that I wouldn't be enjoying this kind of quietude if I had come here after sunset. On most days, after sunset, the garden becomes a venue for "fire shows," accompanied by drum-beats. Young men from nearby areas come here with firecrackers and conduct their shows, mostly for fun. Sometimes they also expect some remuneration from spectators for the fun they provide.

After wandering around the garden for a while, I stopped in front of the monument to the famous Russian painter Ilya Repin (1844-1930). It was installed by the Soviet government on September 29, 1958. The epigraph on the pedestal (as translated into English) reads: "To the great Russian artist Ilya Repin from the government of the Soviet Union."

I was surprised that the Soviet authorities decided to perpetuate Repin's memory with a monument. His attitude toward Soviet power was not all that flattering. The attitude, according to the Russian writer Olga Pigareva, could be gauged from *The Bolsheviks,* one of his paintings. The painting, in her words, depicts "ugly men with crooked smiles rob[bing] a little boy."

I rested for a while on a nearby concrete bench. The Kremlin is only a short distance from there. "Why not visit the Kremlin for one last time, before saying good-bye to Moscow?" I said to myself and headed in that direction.

By the time I reached the Kremlin, it was past 4 p.m. and raining. Though raining, there was a big crowd near the entrance – the same Kutafya Tower gate through which I had entered the complex the day before. Those who had already bought tickets – different units of the complex charged different entrance fees – were rushing to the gate. Others were rushing to the ticket windows. I was surprised that people were buying tickets even though they knew that the place would be closed to visitors at 5 p.m.

Most of them were foreigners. It seemed that even a token visit to the Kremlin was important for them. A tourist to Moscow wouldn't consider his tour complete unless he has visited the Kremlin, even if it is only for a few minutes.

The purpose of my being there was not to pay any perfunctory visit like that. It was to relive the excitement I had felt the day before, when I was face-to-face with monuments and icons representing individuals and events that changed the course of Russia's history. I wouldn't be able to do that in a few minutes, I thought to myself, looking at the long line in front of the ticket windows. I changed my mind about going in. After hanging around for a while, I headed for the nearby metro station.

Russian State Library

As I was walking toward the station, I saw a statue of the legendary Russian novelist Fyodor Dostoevsky at the entrance to a building complex. Only when I entered the complex did I realize that it was the famous Russian State Library. I wondered why our guide didn't even mention it during our tour the day before, when we were only a few yards away from it. It's not just any library. It's the largest library in Russia, and the second-largest in the world, after the Library of Congress in Washington, D.C.

It was founded in 1862 as the Moscow Public Museum and Rumyantsev Museum. The library part of the museum had its origins in the personal collections of Count Nikolai Rumyantsev (1754–1826). It grew rapidly by virtue of its being the legal depository of all publications issued in the Russian Empire and also as a recipient of personal collections donated by prominent Russian scholars, scientists and writers.

In 1925, it was renamed V. I. Lenin State Library of the USSR, in honor of the founding father of the first Communist country in the world. Lenin, after the 1917 Bolshevik Revolution, had played an important role in the library's reorganization, supplementing its original collection with many private collections confiscated by the authorities. In 1992, with the dissolution of the USSR, the name was again changed, this time to the Russian State Library. Most Muscovites still refer to it as the Lenin Library.

The library was closed when I arrived there, and I was disappointed. I had hoped to get at least a glimpse of what the interior of this storied institution, which attracts about 4,000 visitors a day, looks like. It contains, according to *The Columbia Encyclopedia*, more than 42 million items – including some 17 million books and serials, 13 million journals, and 650,000 newspapers – in Russian and 247 other languages.

As I came out of the gate, I took a good look at the Dostoevsky statue. I wondered whether the Russian literary giant, if alive today, would have approved of the idea of a statue commemorating him being placed on the premises of a library, which some Russians sill associate with Lenin's name. Dostoevsky, though respected all over the world for his literary accomplishments, was a Slavophile who believed in the superiority of Slavic, especially Russian, culture and language. The supremacy of the international proletariat, which Lenin believed in and strove to establish, is something Dostoevsky would have detested.

"Two Russian giants, but poles apart in terms of personality." That's what I mulled over as I headed for my hotel.

15

Two Uzbeks Greet Me with Song from Old Hindi Movie

July 27-28, 2009 – Monday-Tuesday

Moscow's international airport is quite far from the city. It takes two-hour subway, plus half-hour surface, train ride to reach the airport. There is no metro, or any other public transportation, service from midnight till 6 a.m. To be on time for an early-morning flight leaving Moscow, one has to leave the city well before midnight. Unless, of course, one is prepared to take a taxi and pay 80 U.S. dollars.

My flight to the Latvian capital of Riga, the next stop on my European tour, was at 7:30 a.m. And I was not prepared to pay 80 dollars for taxi. (That I ended up paying much more, because of a blunder I made, is a different matter. More about the blunder, in a little bit.) So I decided on the other option: public transportation. Which meant that I would have to leave the city well before the metro system shuts down at midnight.

Though I had all day at my disposal, I was reluctant to go into the city and wander around out of fear of being stranded. The possibility of being stranded is always there when one wanders alone in a city he is not familiar with. So I decided to spend the day on the premises of the hotel, doing everything leisurely.

I got out of my hotel room around 10 a.m. My first thought was on a light breakfast. "Breakfast is not included in this," the lady at the reception desk had told me on the first day itself, while collecting three days' rent in advance. I would have to pay for it. Frugal travelers like me find eating at fast-food places less expensive than eating at high-class hotels. There were a few such places, open 24 hours, near the hotel. I walked into one of them.

As I walked in, two middle-aged men working there serenaded me with a song from the old Hindi film *Awara*. The 1951 film, produced and directed by the legendary actor Raj Kapoor, who also played the lead role in it, had been very popular in India. I was elated that two total strangers chose to welcome me in this manner. "So, you have seen *Awara,* eh?" I said.

"Yes," both of them replied, together.

They spoke a little English and also knew a few Hindi words. They told me that they learned those words in their childhood days, when they used to watch a lot of Hindi movies. Hindi movies, they added, were very popular in Tashkent, their home town.

"I know," I told them, "that Hindi movies were, and still are, popular not just in Tashkent, but in many other parts of the former Soviet Union as well. But I never knew that they had this much impact on the people there."

"Oh!" one of them exclaimed. "We loved." He rattled off the names of some of the popular Hindi movies of the 1950s and 1960s he and his friends had seen while growing up in Tashkent.

"We loved Raj Kapoor," his friend added. "We loved Vyjayanthimala."

I could see they were getting sentimental. They were disappointed to hear from me that both Raj Kapoor and Vyjayanthimala were dead and gone. (Years later, I bitterly regretted for having misled the Uzbeks about Vyjayanthimala, when I heard from a friend that she was still alive.)

The two men had left Tashkent, the capital of Uzbekistan, and come to Moscow as teenagers, when their country was one of the republics of the Soviet Union. They decided to stay on in Moscow, even after their country became independent, in 1991, following the breakup of the Soviet Union. Every time they saw an Indian, they told me, their memories would go back to their Tashkent days, when Hindi movies were their only source of entertainment.

"Married? Family?" I asked them.

"I married," one of them said. Pointing to his friend, he added, "He not married. My wife Uzbek. One son."

When I saw that there were other customers waiting in line behind me, I decided to end my conversation. "Nice talking with you," I told them, "I will come back later." I picked up the egg sandwich and coffee that I had ordered and left.

While having my breakfast at the nearby park, my mind was still with the two Uzbeks. "How many such people might have come from all former Soviet republics and made Moscow their home?" I wondered. "Do those non-Russian natives feel at home among Russians who are proud of their ethnicity?"

Chat with a Russian Undergrad

As planned, I checked out of the hotel well before midnight and took the metro to the station from where the express train to the airport leaves. Sitting next to me at the station, waiting for the same express train to the airport, was a young man, maybe in his late teens or early twenties. I was happy that he spoke fairly good English. He also knew a bit of German, he told me. We started chatting. In a few minutes, the train arrived and we continued our chat on the train.

He said he was an undergraduate student at the Moscow State University. He impressed me as one of the new generation of Russians that has been relishing every moment of freedom that came with the end of Communist rule in the country.

"Until recently, we were a closed society," he started opening up. "It will take years for us to catch up with Western Europe. Thank God for the Internet. The authorities may block the channels they don't like. But still we can access some channels and find out what is happening in the rest of the world."

Thanks to the Internet, he was able to secure an invitation to a summer program in Rome. He was on his way to attend the two-week program, organized and paid for by an environmental protection agency.

"I came upon this because of my habit of web surfing," he said. "Our universities don't have programs like this. And because my parents encouraged me to learn English, I am able to take advantage of this program. Most of my classmates know only Russian. Some universities, including mine, have foreign language courses. But they are not that popular. I hope things change soon."

He will be completing his bachelor's degree in physics in another two years. "I am fascinated by history," he said. "I am also fond of traveling. So are my parents. They loved the few days they spent in your country, especially their time in Goa."

By the time we reached the airport, it was past midnight. His flight was at six in the morning and mine at 7:30. We decided to have a coffee at the first airport coffee shop we came across. We continued our conversation for a few more hours. I was flattered when he told me that he learned a lot about India, "thanks to our meeting."

"You already knew a lot about India," I said. "I learned a lot about Russia from you too."

His intellectual curiosity impressed me. Before taking leave of me, he volunteered to walk with me up to the terminal from which Aeroflot operated.

It was a long walk, made longer and more difficult by the construction activities that were going on at the airport. I thanked him for his help and added, "I would have wasted a lot of time locating the terminal on my own."

I didn't see any airport shuttle buses helping passengers move from one terminal to another, as is the case at most international airports. Having had such a long and friendly chat, I felt comfortable enough to tell my new Russian friend what I thought about the airport: "This is the most unorganized international airport I have seen in my life."

"I agree with you," he said, nodding. "I have seen a few European airports by now. Compared with them, this is very primitive. But do come back to Russia. You will see things different next time."

"I will come back," I told him, "if not for anything else, to see how much things have changed for the better since democratic values started trickling in."

When we reached the Aeroflot counter, he said, "I have to go further. Alitalia operates from another terminal."

We exchanged addresses and phone numbers and promised to stay in touch. I gave him a warm hug and thanked him for the wonderful time I had with him. "I wish you all the best," I said. "You will go far in life." He blushed.

A Costly Blunder

And now, to the blunder that I made. I was waiting in line in front of the Aeroflot check-in counter, with my passport and ticket in hand. When I took a casual look at the ticket, I found to my utter shock that I had arrived at the airport a day earlier. This blunder, and the disappointment it caused, could have been avoided if I had done the last thing I always do before leaving for airport or train station: checking the ticket for one last time, even when I knew I had checked it several times before. For reason I am unable to explain, I didn't do it this time. And I felt bitter about it. I withdrew from the line and sat on a nearby bench.

"What to do next?" I started mulling. "Should I go back to the hotel, explain to them what happened and stay there one more day? After all, I have already paid for it."

Of all the places I stayed thus far during this trip, the Ismailovo Hotel was the one I enjoyed the most. That it cost me more than the other places did bother me a little. But the TV in the room, with access to 24-hour BBC News, helped me get over it. For a news junkie like me, it's a big deal. I didn't have that luxury at the other places.

Going back to the city in the morning rush hour, only to spend a few hours there, and then going through the ordeal of getting back to the airport as I have just done didn't seem a good idea. The other option was to check with Aeroflot whether there was any seat available on the flight that would take off in a few minutes. I approached the booking counter.

"There are plenty of vacant seats," the lady at the counter said. "But changing your existing reservation would cost you 150 U.S. dollars."

Thus I ended up paying $150 for changing the flight and losing $160 that I had already paid at the hotel for the day I did not stay there. Add to that the money I was going to pay at the hostel in Riga for the one extra day I would be staying there. The money wasted was quite a bit, especially for a person traveling on a shoestring.

I tried to forget all that, saying to myself, "The wonderful time I had with the Russian student, who gave me an entirely different perspective on his generation's attitude toward their country and the outside world, is the result of the blunder I made. Look at the positive side, you idiot."

16

Musings on How Baltic Breakaway Led to Soviet Breakup

July 28, 2009 – Tuesday

As I was sitting at the Moscow international airport, waiting for the announcement of my flight, another thought began to bother me: "My three-day stay at the hostel in Riga begins only tomorrow. What if the hostel is fully booked for tonight? I will be wandering around in a strange city, looking for a place to stay." I had similar frustrating experiences before, in other cities.

How to contact the hostel in Riga to explain my situation to them? I didn't have the type of cellphone most international travelers carry these days, the type that one can use in most parts of the word. Using a pay phone at the airport and charging the call to one of my credit cards wouldn't be as easy as it is in other big cities. Unless, of course, you know Russian. I had gone through that frustration, too, during my brief stay in Moscow.

When I looked around the waiting area, I saw a young woman who had just finished talking with someone on her cellphone. I approached her and explained my situation. "Could I use your phone to call Riga?" I asked her. "And I don't mean to offend you when I say this: I would like to pay for it."

"Don't worry about paying," she said. "The battery may die any moment. I got the low-battery alert when I was talking.

You can use it as long as the battery lasts." She handed me her phone.

After a couple of minutes' talk with someone at the hostel in Riga, I handed the phone back to her and said, "I don't know whether the woman whom I got on the phone understood anything I said. To everything I said, her answer was yes, not a word more. Thank you very much for your help. By the way, you speak good English."

She laughed and brushed aside my compliment. Then she asked to see the address of the Riga hostel I had just contacted.

"Oh, this is close to the city bus station," she said. "Don't even take a taxi. There are buses from the airport every few minutes. You will be at the bus station in half an hour or so. A few minutes' walk from there, and you are at this hostel. Don't worry. Even if you are lost, Riga is a safe place to wander around."

"You make me feel good," I told her. "I am not nervous anymore." I sat by her side and continued our conversation.

She said she was a Latvian, from Riga, doing her master's at the London School of Economics. "So I have to speak good English," she said with a smile, alluding to my earlier remark about her English. She was on her summer break. After spending a few days with her friends in Moscow, she was "now on my way home in Riga. My parents are anxiously waiting for me. I will be back in London in early September."

I was enjoying the conversation when an announcement on the PA system interrupted it. "They are asking us to board," she said.

On hearing the announcement, a young man came out of the nearby toilet. He rushed toward her and said, "Sorry, darling, it took long."

"This is my boyfriend," she said. "Enjoy your stay in Riga." Both of them walked toward the boarding gate.

I was a little disappointed. I had been hoping to change my seat on the flight, so I could sit next to her and continue chatting with her. Surmising that she and her boyfriend were in their early courting stage, I decided to leave them alone, and stood in line several feet away from them.

The Riga airport is small. It was not at all crowded at the early morning hour we arrived. It looked as though ours was the only flight that arrived at that time. At the baggage-claiming area I once again ran into the young couple.

"Here we go again," the woman said.

As we came out of the airport, she pointed at a bus-stop a few yards away and said, "That's where you get your bus. My parents are picking us up. We are going in a different direction. Otherwise, I would have requested my parents to drop you."

"Don't worry," I told her. "You have already helped me a lot." I paused for a moment and continued, "I pass through London now and then. If you are comfortable about it, let's exchange our email addresses. I will look up for you when I am in London next."

"With pleasure," she said. Apart from her email address, she also wrote down a telephone number and said, "This is my parents' phone number. If you need any help while in Riga, give us a call."

This time, she didn't just walk away. She gave me a hug. Her boyfriend shook hands with me.

"You made my day," I told them and walked toward the bus-stop.

Molotov-Ribbentrop Pact

The bus ride from the airport was very pleasant. Latvia is a sparsely populated country – fewer than 2.2 million people are spread over an area of 24,938 square miles. For a person who lived most of his life in two crowded cities, Mumbai and New York, the morning ride through the almost-empty Latvian streets was an entirely different experience. During the short ride, I also refreshed my memory on some historical facts about Latvia and the other two Baltic States, Estonia and Lithuania.

The first time the three counties aroused my interest was when I heard about the secret protocols to the famous Molotov-Ribbentrop Pact, concluded between the Soviet Union and Nazi Germany on August 23, 1939. The pact, named after the two foreign ministers who signed it, Vyacheslav Mikhailovich Molotov of the Soviet Union and Joachim von Ribbentrop of Germany, was known to the rest of the world as a treaty of nonaggression between the two countries.

The rest of the world did not know, nor did it bother to find out, at the time that there were secret protocols appended to the pact. It was these protocols that virtually divided Eastern Europe into Soviet and German spheres of influence. The three Baltic States and Finland fell into the Soviet sphere. After the outbreak of World War II, on September 1, 1939, the Soviet Union annexed the Baltic States. In 1940, they were reorganized as Soviet republics.

The initial Soviet occupation of the Baltic States lasted less than two years. On June 22, 1941, Germany, in violation of the nonaggression pact, launched Operation Barbarossa. Its goal was to annihilate the Soviet Union. As part of the operation, the Nazis occupied the Baltic States. Initially, the Balts welcomed the Nazis as liberators from Soviet tyranny. But before long, they found out the true color of the Nazis. Their occupation was notorious for discrimination against Jews, mass deportations and killings. After Germany's defeat in World War II, the Soviet Union reoccupied the Baltic States. From 1945, all the way until the breakup of the Soviet Union in 1991, the three Baltic States remained three of the 15 Soviet republics.

The fact that there were secret protocols to the Molotov-Ribbentrop Pact had come to light soon after World War II. But until 1989, the Soviet Union persistently denied their existence. On August 23, 1989, on the 50th anniversary of the pact, approximately two million people from the three Baltic States held a demonstration protesting against their illegal occupation by the Soviet Union. They formed a human chain, called "The Baltic Chain," across the 370-mile stretch of Baltic territories bordering the Soviet Union.

When their demand for independence intensified, Mikhail Gorbachev, the head of the Soviet Union at the time, set up a commission to thoroughly study the Molotov-Ribbentrop Pact. The goal was to find out whether any protocols, in pursuance of which the Soviet Union annexed the Baltic States, existed in the pact.

The commission concluded that they did. It submitted a report to that effect in early December 1989. On December 24, the first democratically elected Congress of Soviets passed a "declaration admitting the existence of the secret protocols, condemning and denouncing them."

The Federal Republic of Germany had made a similar declaration on September 1, 1989.

Those declarations paved the way for the Baltic States to become totally free. On March 11, 1990, Lithuania became the first of the three to proclaim its independence from the Soviet Union. Estonia followed suit on August 20, 1991 and Latvia the next day.

The three states' unilateral declaration of independence met with angry reaction from the Soviet Union. Gorbachev retaliated by cutting off Soviet gas supplies to them. The dispute over gas supplies was resolved later. But there was no going back on the Baltic States' decision to break away from the Soviet Union.

It was the Baltic breakaway that initiated the process of the disintegration of the Soviet Union. The process was completed on December 31, 1991, by which time all the 15 Soviet republics had become independent. The Soviet Union, or the Union of Soviet Socialist Republics, as it was officially called, was no more.

My mental journey through the events in Baltic history that became instrumental in the breakup of the Soviet Union came to an end as I arrived at the Riga bus station.

Arrival in Riga

The lady who welcomed me into the Riga hostel was an ethnic-Russian. A pleasant person, she hardly spoke any English. I immediately knew that she was the one who spoke with me when I called the hostel from the Moscow airport. She said something in Russian, which a student from St. Petersburg, who was staying at the hostel, translated for me into flawless English. The student, an attractive girl, maybe in her late teens or early twenties, said that the lady was apologizing for her inability to speak English. "She teaches Russian at a high school here," the student added. "She is the wife of the hostel owner and helps her husband in her free time."

"No need to apologize," I told her. "I have already heard her speak two languages, Russian with you and Latvian with a few other guests who just passed by. I don't know how many other languages she speaks. And how many people in the world speak even two languages the way she does? Moreover, she is very pleasant."

She gave me a sweet smile when the St. Petersburg student translated to her what I said. She also gave me a special deal. The room I had booked was supposed to be shared by three people. The other two had canceled their booking a few hours earlier. The student explained to me the situation and then added, "She wants me to tell you that if nobody shows up, the whole room is yours."

"That more than makes up for the small difficulty I experienced while talking with her over the phone this morning," I told her.

I made enquiries with the student, who knew Riga very well, and the hostess about some must-see places in the city. When I heard from them that about four hours' bus ride would take me to either of the two other Baltic countries, I decided to turn the blunder I made in checking out of the hotel in Moscow a day earlier into an advantage. I decided to utilize the extra day I gained in Latvia to visit Estonia. I conveyed to them my decision, adding, "Lithuania will have to wait. Or let me see how I feel about it tomorrow."

"Enjoy your stay," the student said. The hostess also said something, which I thought meant the same.

17

Estonia's Capital Still Has an Old-World Charm

July 29, 2009 – Wednesday

I was on my way from Latvia to Estonia. With greenery all around and very few vehicles on the road, I could not have asked for a more enjoyable bus ride. When the bus reached the border between Latvia and Estonia, two lady officers belonging to the Estonian border police came on board. They checked the passports of all the passengers.

I was surprised to see them ask a young woman and an elderly man, sitting in the row in front of me, to get off the bus and follow them. They were taken to the police van parked nearby. I could see through the window of the van that they were being interrogated. After a few minutes, they all came back. The woman was still arguing with the police, in Russian. She opened her pocketbook and took some money out and gave it to the police and got a receipt for it.

She explained to me later, in perfect English, what it was all about: She and her grandfather were citizens of Latvia. Her grandfather did not have his passport with him. For identification, he was carrying his driver's license. He did not carry the passport because he was under the impression that, since Latvia became part of the European Union, a Latvian could travel to all EU countries, including Estonia, without a passport.

I told her that I was also under the same impression. "Maybe, because the Baltic States joined the EU only recently, not all EU regulations, especially the travel-related ones, have been implemented as yet," I said. "It seems the border police are still following the old regulations."

The young lady was visibly upset. "Had I known this, I wouldn't have put my grandfather through all this trouble," she said. "I finished college last year. This is my first vacation since I started working. I wanted to give my grandpa a good treat. And some treat, this one. They charged me a 15-lat fine."

She was referring to the Latvian lat (LVL), the currency of the country. The fine would come to about 20 euros. "It's not the amount of money that's at issue here," she added. "It's the way they treated us. They treated us like criminals."

Though the fine was imposed by the Estonian authorities, they did not insist that it be paid in their currency, the Estonian kroon (EEK). They had no problem collecting it in Latvian lat.

Baltic Integration in the EU

All three Baltic States had initiated the process of switching to euro soon after they joined the European Union. To get slightly ahead of our story, Estonia completed the process and joined the Eurozone on January 1, 2011. Latvia did it on January 1, 2014 and Lithuania on January 1, 2015.

The Baltic States were admitted to the European Union on May 1, 2004. A country would attain legal status as a member only when it ratifies the treaties that were the constitutional basis of the EU: the Treaty on the European Union (the Maastricht Treaty of 1991) and the Treaty Establishing the European Community (the Rome Treaty of 1957). By the time the Baltic States began their ratification processes, the two treaties had already been amended and replaced with the Treaty of Lisbon. Latvia ratified the Lisbon Treaty on June 16, 2008; Lithuania on August 26,

2008; and Estonia on September 23, 2008. The Treaty of Lisbon came into force on December 1, 2009, with the last hold-over country, the Czech Republic, ratifying it on November 3, 2009.

So the Latvian lady's anger was understandable. After all, the citizens of all member states of the EU had been told that a major advantage of being part of the union was the freedom they would be enjoying to travel among all member states as though they constituted one country. Even a year after her country completed all legal formalities to become a member of the EU, she was denied that freedom – that, too, at the border between her country and Estonia, both of which were parts of one country, the Soviet Union, until a few years ago.

After that unpleasant interruption, the bus resumed its journey. The argument now was between the Latvian woman and her grandfather. I couldn't tell what it was about. I had started having my breakfast, which I had picked up at Riga before boarding the bus. I craned my neck toward the woman and said, "Let not that small incident ruin your trip."

She just smiled, but continued her argument.

After a couple of minutes, I tapped her shoulder and said, "Please have some orange juice." I offered the large cup of orange juice, half of which I had already drunk.

"No, I am fine," she said. "Thank you, though."

"I won't be able to finish it anyway," I told her. "I don't want to waste it. After that heated exchange with the police, you need something to cool yourself."

She thanked me and took it.

Exploring Tallinn with a Russian

After two more hours of ride, the bus reached Tallinn, the capital of Estonia. A young man who was getting off the bus with me smiled at me. "Have we met before?" I asked him.

He said he had overheard my conversation with the hostel owner's wife the day before. He was staying at the same hostel.

The young man, tall and handsome, spoke enough English to make himself understood.

He told me that he was on a week's vacation from his work in Russia. He worked as a cop, on desk duty, in a small Russian town bordering on Finland. He was also on a tight schedule, he said. Like me, he would be returning to Riga in the evening. When I suggested that we explore Tallinn together, he happily agreed to it. He said he would be making a similar trip to Vilnius, the capital of Lithuania, the net day.

"I will join you if my energy level permits," I told him. "I will let you know in the evening."

His jovial mood and friendliness helped me overcome, in a matter of minutes, the language barrier between us. At the Tallinn bus station, we picked up some travel brochures and marked a few important places we thought we should visit in the few hours we had at our disposal. One of the brochures said, "This is certainly not a place for a fleeting visit: with so much on offer you'd be doing the town, and yourself, a disservice."

I thought the warning was especially meant for people like me.

We were in Tallinn Old Town, the area of the city that still has buildings of medieval architecture. The travel brochure was exaggerating only slightly when it described the place as "mystic, addictive and mesmerizing." The place does have an old-world charm. Some of the buildings date back to the 11th century. Often referred to as the "medieval pearl of Europe," Tallinn Old Town got classified by the UNESCO, in 1997, as a World Cultural Heritage Site.

The name *Tallinn* has a Danish origin. The area of Estonia that became Tallinn was conquered by the Danish King Waldemar II, in 1219. It happened during the Northern Crusades. Danes started settling in the new land conquered by their king, and the town they built around their settlement came to be called *Taani linn,* which, in Estonian, means Danish town. *Tallinn* is derived from *Taani linn.*

By 1227, all of Estonia had come under German control.

When Tallinn joined the German-dominated Hanseatic League, in 1285, it became a channel for trade between Novgorod, an important trade and cultural center in Russia at the time, and the West. It flourished as a marketplace for traders until the mid-16th century. That, until 1918, Tallinn was also referred to by its German name, Reval, is a testimony to the important role the German settlers played in its growth. The Germans were mostly artisans and merchants.

The story of Tallinn, and of most of Estonia, from early 13th century to early 20th century, is one of domination by Denmark, Germany, Sweden and Russia. With brief interruptions now and then, Russia was in control of Estonia for nearly two centuries. From 1945 to 1991, to repeat what we said in the previous chapter, it was one of the constituent republics of the Soviet Union.

Though Estonia broke away from the Soviet Union in 1991, the impact Soviet rule had on the country is likely to last forever. It is the outcome of the Russification policy the Soviet Union followed in all its newly-grabbed lands. Today, 25 percent of Estonia's 1.3-million population is ethnically Russian. The Russian language is widely used in the country.

"Maharaja India Restoran"

My Russian friend and I were in Town Hall Square – *Raekoja plats,* in the Estonian language. A signboard, with "Maharaja India Restoran" written on it in large letters, was staring at me from the other side of the square. "Let's go and see what the inside looks like," I told the Russian. "It's too early for lunch. We'll decide where to have lunch later."

There were no customers inside. Two Estonian waitresses were setting up the place for lunch. I asked one of them whether the place was actually Indian-owned. "Yes, he is the owner," she said, pointing to a smart-looking Sikh, in a white suit and red turban, sitting on a high stool in the bar section of the restaurant. He could be in his late forties or early fifties. He walked toward us, beaming, and introduced himself: "Ajit Singh." Then he turned to his employees and said something.

"Do you speak Estonian?" I asked him.

"No, I spoke Russian just now," he said. "I learned Russian after coming to Estonia. I learned it from my employees. I didn't go to JNU to learn it, as most of my friends did."

He was referring to the famous Jawaharlal Nehru University of New Delhi. The courses in Russian offered by JNU are very popular in India.

Ajit Singh opened his restaurant in 1991. According to him, there are about 150 Indians living in all of Estonia. "We have an Indian consulate here in Tallinn, no embassy," he said. "The consulate is attached to the Indian embassy in the Finnish capital of Helsinki. Helsinki is only two hours by boat. Latvia and Lithuania also have only consulates, no embassies yet. Their consulates, in Riga and Vilnius, function under the jurisdiction of the Indian embassy in Sweden."

Mr. Singh said that he was originally from Jalandhar, Punjab, but spent several years in New Delhi before coming to Estonia. Then he took a good look at me and said, with a smile, "I can tell you are from the South. Tamil Nadu or Kerala?"

"There is no mistaking of that. I am from Kerala."

"Oh, I have many friends from Kerala. They work for Nokia, across the gulf."

He was referring to the Gulf of Finland. Nokia Corporation, the leading mobile phone maker in the world, has its headquarters in Finland.

"Do you know that Nokia's largest manufacturing facility is in India?" I asked him.

"Yes, I know that," he replied.

Though there was not a single customer inside, the décor and furniture of the restaurant gave me the impression that it had seen some prosperous times. During their boom period (2000-2006), the Baltic States were nicknamed Baltic Tigers, an allusion to the Asian Tigers. The rapid economic growth, which the Asian Tigers – Hong Kong, Taiwan, Singapore and South

Korea – experienced between the early 1960s and the 1990s, was the envy of the rest of the world at that time.

As the birthplace of Skype, Estonia had become a major beneficiary of the boom in information technology. But the global financial crisis of 2008 hit the Baltic States very hard. Estonia's growth rate, which had been over 11 percent in 2006, fell to 3.6 percent. The government in Latvia collapsed in the wake of the crisis. The new government, under Prime Minister Valdis Dombrovskis, took over in March 2009. Did the crisis affect Mr. Singh's restaurant business?

"Not as badly as other businesses," he said. "Most of my customers are tourists. As you know, tourists are not as tightfisted as the local people. But because the economic crunch has hurt tourism, my business also has slowed down. We'll get over it."

"I like that optimism," I told him. "I wish you all the best."

When my friend and I got up to leave, he stopped us and said, "No, you can't leave like that. You must have something. Coffee, tea or some juice?"

"I have heard a lot about Indian hospitality," my Russian friend said. Mr. Singh and I brushed it off with a smile.

"It is very hot outside," I said. "A glass of water will be ideal."

Mr. Singh went behind the bar table and filled two glasses from a tap. "Yes, today is unusually hot," he said, handing us the glasses.

"We have only a few hours left before we take our bus back to Riga," I told him. "We want to go around and see as much of Tallinn as we can before we leave. Otherwise, we would have stayed for lunch."

We shook hands with Mr. Singh, thanked him and left.

Hare Krishna Followers of Tallinn

Town Hall Square is known as the "social heart" of Tallinn. Free music concerts are held here on most summer evenings. We were told that all the empty outdoor cafes we were seeing would be filled with customers by evening. In December, the square gets "transformed into a charming Christmas Market," according to one of the travel brochures.

The square is also famous for its summer fairs. Something that could pass for a fair was going on when we passed by. Estonians who had fallen on hard times were out there selling things, most of them made by themselves – children's clothes and toys, paintings, photographs, picture frames, etc. We walked past all of them, but we couldn't help stopping at a table with a variety of chocolates spread on it. It was not the chocolates that made us stop, though. It was the two girls selling them that did it. They were very attractive. The chocolates were homemade, they said. They also said that they were selling them partly to pay for their college. I felt obligated to buy some.

When I tried to take a picture of them, my Russian friend grabbed my camera and insisted that I pose between the two girls. They happily obliged. Standing between them, I said, "This is my souvenir from Estonia."

"You are welcome, Sir," one of the girls said.

When I heard a sound of music wafting in from a distance, it aroused my curiosity. It was the sound not just of any music, but Indian music. I was not expecting Indian music in a small Baltic town where I had not seen a single Indian, except a restaurant owner. "Let's go and take a look," I told my Russian friend, pointing to an alley out of which the music came.

As we reached near the alley, we saw a bunch of Hare Krishna followers emerging from it. All of them were men, in their late twenties or early thirties. All were clad in loincloth and kurta, some saffron-colored and some white. A few of them banged cymbals, one played on the *tabla* (the Indian percussion instrument) and another one on the harmonium. All of them chanted:

Hare Rama, hare Rama, Rama Rama, hare hare;
Hare Krishna, Hare Krishna, Krishna Krishna, hare hare.

My Thirty-Day European Odyssey

They came out of one alley, crossed the square and went into another alley. We watched them until they disappeared from our sight.

"Do you have them in your town?" I asked my friend.

"No," he said. "I have heard about them. This is the first time I am seeing them in person."

"They are there in all big cities of the world," I said. "I didn't expect them in Tallinn. This is America's contribution to Hinduism."

We continued our exploration of the Old Town area. We passed by several churches, most of them small, blending well with other buildings. St. Olaf's Church, named after the Norwegian King Olav Haraldsson, is an exception. It dwarfs all other buildings in the area.

The original structure, built by Danish settlers as a place for socializing and worshiping, underwent renovation and rebuilding a few times. It was burned down three times and its steeple was hit by lightning 10 times. When the steeple was raised to the height of 159 meters, around the year 1500, it became the tallest structure in the world. Since then, needless to say, many other structures have come up around the world, surpassing it in height. It still dominates the Tallinn skyline.

From 1945 to 1991, when Estonia was part of the Soviet Union, the tower of St. Olaf's Church came in handy for its security apparatus, the K.G.B. It used it as a radio tower and installed surveillance equipment on its spire.

Another important landmark in Old Town Tallinn is St. Nicholas Church. It was built by German settlers around 1230. The interior of this sturdy structure, "designed to double as a fortress" before the Germans built a wall around their new settlements, was almost destroyed in World War II Soviet bombings. The restored structure is now used more as a museum and music hall than as a place of worship. It houses the Niguliste Art Museum of Estonia. The most popular piece of art in the museum is *Danse Macabre* (the Dance of Death), painted by

Bernt Notke at the end of the 15th century. The music hall is much-sought-after by concert organizers.

My Russian friend and I had only a couple of hours left. So we decided to go up the hill, to the part of the town called Toompea. *Toompea* is derived from the German word *Domberg*, meaning the Cathedral Hill. The cathedral from which the hill gets its name is the Aleksandr Nevsky Cathedral. Famous for its golden-onion rooftops and luxurious interiors, this biggest Greek Orthodox church in Tallinn is another important landmark in the city. There was a time when it was mandatory for women to cover their hair while entering the cathedral. Not anymore.

Toompea is also the seat of the government of Estonia. The Toompea Castle, whose original structure was built in 1227 by the German Knights of the Sword, now houses Estonia's parliament. A few yards away is the Stenbock House. Named after Count Jakob Pontus Stenbock, a descendant of a Swedish noble family who completed most of its construction in 1787, it is now the office of the prime minister. It was originally meant to be a courthouse.

We had been strongly recommended not to leave Toompea before taking in the spectacular view of Tallinn from its top. The view of Old Town with its medieval red rooftops, juxtaposed with the modern city center, was spectacular. The coastline at a distance added to the beauty.

"All good things come to an end abruptly," I told my Russian friend, looking at the watch. We had only a few minutes left to catch the 7 p.m. bus we were booked on. We climbed down the hill and walked fast. Destination: *TALLINNA BUSSIJAAM*.

18

Tour of Latvian Capital; Lunch with a German-Thai Guilty of Being Rich

July 30, 2009 – Thursday

Latvia's early history is similar to that of Estonia. Both were subjected to attack and conquest by the powers that led the Northern Crusades, also known as the Baltic Crusades. Riga, the capital of Latvia, was founded in 1201 by Teutonic (Germanic) colonists. It became a strategic base for the Crusaders, especially the Livonian Brothers of the Sword. Like Tallinn, Riga also became a principal trading center in the German-controlled Hanseatic League. Because of its strategic location and prosperity, it also became a bone of contention among four major powers of the time: the State of the Teutonic Order (later Germany), the Polish-Lithuanian Commonwealth, Sweden and Russia. The longest period of its domination by a foreign power began in 1710, when the control over Riga switched from Sweden to Russia. By the end of the 19th century, thanks to its rapid industrialization, Latvia became one of the most developed parts of the Russian Empire.

The prosperity also gave rise to Latvian nationalism. What began in the 1850s as a murmuring discontent against Russian domination, played out in full force during the civil war that broke out in Russia in the wake of the Bolshevik Revolution.

Latvians' prolonged struggle to break away from the Russian Empire culminated in its total independence, in 1920.

Unfortunately, the independence proved to be short-lived. As we discussed in Chapter 16, soon after World War II broke out in 1939, Latvia and the other two Baltic States – Estonia and Lithuania – were annexed by the Soviet Union. (Russia, together with the territories it grabbed after Communist rule was firmly established in the country, had been renamed the Union of Soviet Socialist Republics (U.S.S.R.) or the Soviet Union, in 1922.) In 1941, as part of Operation Barbarossa, Germany ousted the Soviet Union from the Baltic States and established its own rule there. After Germany's defeat in World War II, the Soviet Union reoccupied all three states and reconstituted them as Soviet republics.

For nearly half a century, Latvian nationalism remained in a dormant state. It began to resurge in 1985, when Mikhail Gorbachev became the supreme leader of the Soviet Union. The three Baltic States took full advantage of the new policies introduced by Gorbachev. Though the policies, known as *glasnost* (openness) and *perestroika* (restructuring), were aimed at economic and political revitalization of the Soviet Union, they had unanticipated consequences: They led to the unraveling of the country. The Baltic States, to repeat what was said in Chapter 16, were the first to break away. When they declared their independence, one by one, and when other countries of the world started recognizing their independence, the Soviet Union was left with no option but to acquiesce in.

The foregoing history of the Baltic States came back to mind, as I set out to explore Riga, on July 30, 2009. I got out of my hostel at about 9 a.m., with no particular destination in mind. The tour of the city I had booked would start only at 11 a.m.

When I passed by a travel agency on the next block, a display ad on its window caught my attention. The ad announced conducted tours to India and featured an Odissi dancer, in full costume and in a beautiful pose. Could the travel agency be Indian-owned? I went in to find out.

There was only one desk and one employee inside. The employee – a young, attractive Latvian woman – told me that the travel agency was not Indian-owned. It conducted tours to India every summer, if an adequate number of tourists registered for it. "It's already July 30," the Latvian lady added, "and none has registered so far. So no tour is likely this summer."

Like Estonia, Latvia also was experiencing a severe economic crunch. Business was slow in all sectors of the economy. When the economy slows down, tourism is among the sectors that feel the pinch first. The depressing news notwithstanding, I came out of the agency feeling good. Maybe it had to do with the woman I just spoke with. Or maybe it had to do with the display ad on the window. The Indian dancer featured in it, with the Taj Mahal in the background, was so beautiful that anyone would want to take a second look at the ad. The ad did India proud.

I had more than an hour to pass before taking the 11 a.m. tour. The tour was to start outside Stockmann, which I was told was the largest department store in Riga. It was two blocks away from where I was. I decided to spend the remaining time window-shopping at Stockmann.

Compared with the department stores I had been to in many major cities of the world, this one, with only four floors, did not look all that large. It's quite possible that the four-story limit had to do with the building regulations in this environmentally-conscious city. The absence of offensive skyscrapers adds to the beauty of Riga.

Once inside Stockmann, I realized that, in terms of the variety of goods and services sold, it could compete with any department store anywhere in the world. Looking at the employees of the store, I couldn't tell whether they were Latvians or Russians. They spoke with me in English. But while dealing with local customers, they switched between Latvian and Russian, depending on what language the customer spoke. During the short time I was in the store, I heard more Russian than Latvian. It has been said that "Riga is the most Soviet-feeling Baltic capital city." Two-thirds of the city's population is ethnic-Russian. In the country as a whole, Russians make up 40 percent of the population. Very few of them have acquired Latvian citizenship. That makes the Latvian ethnic mix potentially very explosive, according to some demographic analysts. It didn't reach that level in the other two states. In Estonia, Russians make up 26 percent of the population and, in Lithuania, they are a negligible 6 percent.

It was 11 a.m. The tour bus waiting outside Stockmann was about to leave. I rushed to it.

January 13 Street

The bus was packed and I could tell that I was the only Indian on it. I sat near a person and introduced myself. "I had been to India twice," he said. I was surprised to hear that he was from Thailand. He didn't look like a Thai at all. I decided not to mention it right away. I would have plenty of time to clarify it, I said to myself.

The bus soon entered a street called January 13 Street. It's named so, the tour guide said, in memory of those killed during a massive protest rally on the street, on January 13, 1905. Industrial workers and peasants of Riga were protesting against the massacre of their brethren that took place in St. Petersburg, on January 9, 1905. (See "Bloody Sunday 1905," discussed in Chapter 8.) The rally in Riga, too, was dealt with by the authorities the same way the one in St. Petersburg was. When police opened fire, many of the protesters jumped into the icy waters of the nearby Daugava River and drowned. According to one estimate, 73 demonstrators were killed and 200 wounded. No figure is available on those who drowned. Apart from January 13 Street, there is also an impressive statue, on the banks of the Daugava, that commemorates the notorious January 13, 1905, incident.

When the tour bus reached the city hall, the guide gave us a brief history of the imposing statue in front of it. The statue, of two soldiers, has "LATVIESU STRELNIEKI 1915-1920" engraved on it. *Latviesu Strelnieki*, meaning Latvian Riflemen, was created in Latvia, in 1915, as a unit of the Imperial Russian Army. The mission of the unit, consisting mainly of recruits from Latvia, was to defend Baltic territories against the invading German army, during World War I. The Latvians' resentment against Germans goes back to the 13th century when they were conquered by the German-dominated Livonian Order. The resentment increased when the German settlers of Latvia became landowners and part of the governing elite. Later, after the Russian conquest of Latvia and systematic Russification of the land, the resentment was directed against the Russian settlers.

During the Bolshevik Revolution, many members of the Latvian Riflemen unit found common cause with the Bolsheviks and joined in their fight against the czarist regime. So the tall monument we see in front of the city hall is in memory as much of the soldiers who fought against Germans as of those who did against the czar of Russia.

Next, the tour bus passed by the Castle of Riga, which is now the residence of Latvia's president; St. Peter's Church, which has a 153-meter-tall steeple; St. Mary's Catholic Church (the name was changed to Lutheran Cathedral when Latvia came under Swedish rule); the Trinity Orthodox Church; the Latvian National Theater; the Freedom Monument (42 meters high); and many other landmarks, the names of which the tour guide rattled off. When the bus passed through the most elite neighborhood of Latvia, the guide said that it was still known as the Russian suburb. Many streets in the neighborhood have Russian names. One of them is Muskova Street. Russian merchants and Jews settled down in the area generations ago.

One couldn't help noticing the pro-Russian, anti-Latvian-nationalist slant in our guide's commentary. One could easily make out that he was one of those who were opposed to Latvia's breakup with the Soviet Union. He even became nostalgic whenever he referred to the country's Russian past, and described Russian things around. When his commentary became too pro-Russian, the Thai gentleman sitting next to me gave me a nudge and said, "Did you hear that?"

"You can see that type in every country," I told him. "We have Indians who masquerade as more British than the British. They are still nostalgic about the days of the Raj. We call them brown sahibs. We have characters in Goa, the former Portuguese colony, who still hold grudge against India for having liberated them from Portuguese rule."

How the Thai Got European Features

After the tour ended, at about 3 p.m., I told the Thai gentleman that I was very hungry. "Why don't you join me and have something?" I said.

We walked into a nearby pizzeria. Over pizza and coke, we had a long conversation. He opened up when I told him, "You can never pass for an ethnic-Thai. I took you for a Scandinavian or German."

"You are absolutely right," he said, and went on to narrate the story of his mixed origins.

He had a German father and Thai mother. His father had fought in World War II. I didn't want to embarrass him with the question whether his father was a Nazi soldier. It was obvious that he was. After the war, he decided to take a long break and wandered around Southeast Asia. The country where he spent most of his time was Thailand. A few months into his stay in Thailand, he met a Thai woman and married her.

"I got the looks of my German father," he said. "Both my father and mother are dead now."

He had his college education, partly in Germany and partly in the U.S. He specialized in computer programming. When he sold a program that he invented to an American company, he came into big money. He didn't tell me which company he sold it to and how much he sold it for. He might have made a fortune. Or else he wouldn't have quit the job he had in Bangkok to spend the rest of his life pursuing his "life's dream" of traveling around the world. He was on a three-month land tour, from Bangkok to Lithuania. He had already passed through Myanmar, Mongolia, China and Tibet.

"In Tibet, I found more Chinese than Tibetans," he said.

"Tibetans resent it," I told him. "You read about frequent protest demonstrations against Chinese domination of Tibet. Some protesters are even resorting to self-immolation. But there is no let-up in the Chinese attitude. According to the Chinese, Tibet is part of China. I am sure you are aware that the Tibetans' spiritual leader, the Dalai Lama, has been living in India ever since the Chines overran his country in 1957. How much impact can he have when he protests from outside? Moreover, lately, his protests have been somewhat muted."

The Thai-German was in full agreement with my views on Tibet. I decided to veer our conversation back to where we left off, when he mentioned his life's dream. "You said you are on a tour by land from Bangkok to Lithuania," I said. "Are you going to fly back to Bangkok from Lithuania?"

"Not immediately," he said. "From Lithuania, I will be flying to Prague, from there to Berlin and, from Berlin, back to Bangkok."

"I envy you," I told him. "The dream that you are pursuing is my dream too. The only difference is that I am not able to do it as often, and as free of financial worries, as you are. During the past ten years, I have traveled extensively. I return from every travel completely broke."

When he took his video camera off his shoulders and placed it on the table, I couldn't help noticing some exotic features on it. I had never seen such a camera before, and I told him so.

"Yes, it's an expensive camera," he said. "It cost me six thousand euros. With this, I have been documenting my experience all over the world. There was one place where my conscience wouldn't permit me to do it."

"Which place was that?" I asked him.

"The slum of Mumbai," he said. "It was early in the morning."

"Oh, no," I said to myself. I feared that he was going to

give a graphic description of what he might have seen at Mumbai's Dharavi, the largest slum in Asia. Foreigners have talked and written about it, some amusingly, and others, to the embarrassment of most Indians. Indians themselves avoid going through that area in early-morning hours. That's the time the open spaces in the Dharavi slum turn into public toilets. I felt relieved when he started talking about some other aspect of Dharavi.

"The man who was my guide during the three days I spent in Mumbai picked me at the airport," he said. "When we reached the slum area, he said that the film *The Slum Dog Millionaire* was shot there. When I saw people sleeping on wooden benches outside their shacks, I put my camera back into my bag. I said to myself that with the money I spent on this camera, I could easily feed a few families like these for more than a year."

"But," I replied, "don't you agree that the first step toward solving those problems is to make the world aware of them. Your camera would play a useful role in doing it."

"Maybe you have a point," he said. "The problem I have can be called guilt. There was a time when I had five cars, including a Mercedes and a Porsche, and a twenty-two-room house. I was not at all happy. Even a scratch on one of my expensive cars would keep me upset all day. Now I have just one car, a Toyota, and a three-bedroom apartment. I am very, very happy. I carry this camera out of necessity. I try not to use it in places where its use could be mistaken for flaunting."

I nodded in agreement. I could tell that he was not the flaunting type. When the waitress brought the check, I offered to pay for both of us. "No," he said. "Why should you? We'll split the bill."

We exchanged our addresses, promised to stay in touch and said good-bye to each other.

I walked toward my hostel, but my mind was still on some of the things the Thai-German said: about his finding happiness when he traded his ostentatious living for a simple one; and about the guilt he felt when he saw the wretched condition in the Mumbai slum. I have heard similar stories from many Westerners. That has been the motivating factor behind many of them turning philanthropic. I wished he too had turned his guilt into a worthy cause.

"Wasn't it guilt-feeling that made Alfred Nobel the founder of the Nobel Prizes?" I asked myself.

After an hour's rest in my hostel room, I went out again. It was my last day in Riga, and I wanted to enjoy everything around as long as I had the energy to walk. I walked toward the Daugava River.

The Daugava, which empties into the Baltic Sea, has played an important role in Riga's growth and development as a port city. The river has been a transportation route to Central Europe for centuries. Riga's importance as a port city goes back to the days of the Vikings (from the eighth to the tenth century). Since Latvia's independence from the Soviet Union, there have been regular ferry services between Riga and the Swedish capital of Stockholm. Cruise ships and private yachts arrive regularly from Stockholm. With about 4,000 vessels arriving every year, Riga has once again become the bustling port city it once was.

I walked a short distance on the Suspension Bridge over the Daugava, just to get a feel of it. As I had been told that there was nothing important to see on the other side, I returned to the Old Town side. When I reached Stockmann, again, I decided to go in to take one last look.

Next to Stockmann is the largest supermarket in Riga. Next to it is the train station from where one can take trains to all parts of Europe. I spent the remainder of the evening in the area, feeling a little sad that my stay in Riga was coming to an end.

I was tired and it was time for me to head back to the hostel. I went into the supermarket to pick up a beer, but was disappointed to learn that all stores in Riga were prohibited to sell alcohol after 9 p.m. Though disappointed, I did express to the manager of the store my appreciation for the city rule. Not that I had witnessed any untoward alcohol-related incidents on any street. "I wish Moscow and St. Petersburg had similar rules," I told the manager.

He smiled.

Tandoori Chicken at Riga Fast-Food Place

My disappointment at not being able to have a beer didn't last long, though. The next thing I wanted to pick up was something light to eat. When I saw a menu, with "Tandoori Chicken" in bold letters, displayed on the window of a fast-food restaurant, I thought I found exactly what I was looking for. I went in.

To my pleasant surprise, I saw two Indians working in the grill area of the place. I asked them whether the place was Indian-owned.

"No," one of them said. "This is a franchise, with branches in Moscow and St. Petersburg. The franchisee here is Indian. He is from New Delhi."

"And which part of India are you from?" I asked them.

"I am from Bangalore," one of them said. Pointing at the other, he added, "He is from Mumbai."

"I have lived in both places," I told them. "I am originally from Kerala."

We chatted for a while. In fact, they were the only Indians I met in Riga. Their families lived back in India. "Are you happy here?" I asked them.

"So-so," the man from Bangalore said. "The money is OK."

After a few more minutes' chat, I asked him to help me order "something light. I can't eat anything heavy," I told him. "I have to get up early in the morning. I am leaving for Warsaw tomorrow."

He suggested salad with a few pieces of chicken. When I said yes, he placed the order for me with a waitress standing nearby.

"Oh, you speak Latvian, eh?" I said to him.

"Yes, I do," he said. "But what I spoke just now is Russian.

She is from Moscow. I spent two years in Moscow before coming here."

"You have had a colorful life," I said and shook hands with him.

The waitress arrived with my take-out food. The price was very reasonable. It was quite possible that my Indian connection got me a special deal.

I headed to my hostel, feeling great.

19

'Sitar Draws Out the Best in Me,' Says a German: My First Day in Warsaw

July 31, 2009 – Friday

I was on my way from the Warsaw international airport to the hostel where I was going to stay. The public-transportation bus that I took was filled to capacity. I had to travel standing. Standing next to me were two young men with large suitcases.

"Are you tourists?" I asked them.

"No, we are college students from Uzbekistan," one of them said. "We just landed here. We are on our way to the University of Warsaw, where we'll be studying for one year. We are on a student-exchange program."

"Are you from Tashkent?" I asked them.

"Yes," both of them said.

I told them about the two people from Tashkent I met at a fast-food place in Moscow. "I remember them not because of the food they gave me. I do it because they greeted me with a song from an old Hindi movie."

"Yes, Hindi movies are very popular in Uzbekistan," one of them said.

"Especially in the capital," the other one added.

"Can you also sing Hindi songs?" I asked.

"Yes, but not now," the first one said.

My Thirty-Day European Odyssey

He almost ended up studying computer science in India, he told me. "In fact, I had been enthusiastically looking forward to doing it," he added. "At the last moment, the Indian embassy in Tashkent raised some objections and refused to give me a visa. I was very disappointed."

"Try again," I told him. "You will be lucky next time."

The two Uzbeks had to get off at the next stop, and our conversation ended abruptly.

A few minutes later, the bus arrived at the stop where I had to get off. According to the travel instructions provided by the hostel, it was at walking distance from that stop. Two passersby whom I asked for direction did not speak English. A third person who spoke a little English, drew the direction on a piece of paper.

Another person, shabbily dressed and with a few days' growth of beard on his face, took a look at what was drawn on the paper and gestured to me to follow him. I was a little reluctant to accept his offer, because he looked suspicious. I didn't want to be seen in the company of a questionable character, on my very first day in a new place. But because the streets were full of people and the day was still young, I decided to follow him. I knew I would back off if he led me into any deserted area.

We walked several blocks, and the new self-appointed guide didn't seem to know where the hostel was. The man who drew the map showing the direction had told me that it was close by. After a few more minutes' aimless walk, I stopped the 'guide' and stood in front of him to ask whether he knew where he was going. When I was greeted with the stench of alcohol and sweat, I realized that he had taken me for a ride.

Another passerby told me that I was well past the hostel. I had to go back. I told the drunk to "get lost," which I didn't think he understood, and started walking back.

He followed me demanding payment for his 'service.' I shouted at him, but to no avail. He kept pestering me, until I placed a two-euro coin in his hand. I watched him walk away.

A young couple who were enjoying the scene smiled at me. "Every city has this kind," I said. They nodded in agreement.

The courtesy and friendliness of the staff at the hostel more than made up for the annoyance caused by the drunken 'guide.' The young woman who completed the check-in formalities spoke good English. She was a graduate student, studying business and working part-time at the hostel.

"Do you speak Russian as well as you speak English?" I asked her.

She threw a contemptuous look at me. "No," she said. "And I don't want to do it either. I will learn French. I will learn German. I am already taking classes to improve my English. My parents were forced to learn Russian. For that reason alone, I refuse to learn it."

What a pity! The present generation in Poland detests the Russian language, which is as rich as any other language in the word, simply because of what the Soviet Union (and, before that, czarist Russia) had done to their country. The latter continually tried to keep the Poles subjugated.

Russo-Polish Rivalry

The Russo-Polish rivalry dates back to the early 17th century. Poland, at the time, was the dominant partner of the Polish-Lithuanian Commonwealth and Russia was ruled by czars. Czarist Russia's constant meddling in the internal affairs of Poland resulted in the Polish-Muscovite War of 1605-1618. The war ended without any major change in the status quo. But the end of the second conflict between the two, the Russo-Polish War of 1654-1677, marked the beginning of the rise of Russia as a great power in Eastern Europe. Every time Poland got partitioned – the main partitioning occurred in 1772, 1793 and 1795 – it resulted in territorial gains for Russia. In fact, from the beginning of the 1654-1677 war, all the way until 1991, the destiny of Poland had been controlled first by czarist Russia and then by the Communist Soviet Union.

Like any people under foreign domination, Poles resented that control. The resentment continues even now, years after

Poland ceased to be a Soviet satellite. The words of the young lady who checked me in at the hostel bear evidence to it.

After a quick shower and a short nap, I came out of the hostel. I wanted to pick up something to eat. It was already 8 p.m., and I was very hungry.

A young man I ran into outside the hostel told me that there was a Chinese restaurant nearby. He insisted on walking with me to show the place. The actual reason why he insisted, I found out in a few seconds, was that he wanted to talk about India. His friends were traveling around India at the time, and he had been receiving emails from them every day about their exciting experiences in India.

"I couldn't join them this time," he said. "I will surely go there next year."

"Where did you learn to speak English this well?" I asked him.

"At college," he said. "Only my generation does it. My father's generation spoke only Polish and Russian. We realized what my father's generation was missing. In my case, I am a computer science major. I have just started working for an IT company. We use English extensively in our office, especially while dealing with various parties around the world."

When we reached the front of the Chinese restaurant, he wished me a "pleasant stay in Warsaw" and shook hands with me.

I firmly held his hand for a few seconds and said, "Keep up this attitude. You will go far in life. I wish you all the best."

As I entered the hostel kitchen with the simple Chinese dinner – "Hunan Chicken and Rice" – I had bought, I was greeted with another pleasant surprise: the smell of Indian food.

"Who is into Indian cooking here?" I asked two young men who were standing at the kitchen stove and stirring their food. They looked 20-something, one slightly younger than the other.

"I am," the younger one replied.

"Oh, I made a mistake," I said. "I should have come here

before I went out to pick up this Chinese food. I would have found a way of getting invited by you to share your food."

"We are inviting you now," he said. "Please come and join us."

Pointing to a huge fridge in the corner of the kitchen, his friend added, "Keep your Chinese food there. You can eat it tomorrow. We are Germans. We would welcome a certificate from an Indian on the authenticity of our Indian cooking."

"It's very kind of you," I said. "I will join you tomorrow. I am famished right now. I have no patience to wait until you finish your cooking. But when you are done, please come and talk with me. I will wait for you."

By the time they came and sat at my table, I had finished my food. I also had a couple of beers. So when they opened the wine bottle and invited me to join them, I had to "regretfully" decline. "I will take a rain check," I told them. "I will more than make up for what I am denying myself today."

"We'll take you up on that threat," the older one said.

"You'll be sorry."

"Never," his friend replied.

"Tell me," I said, "what got you interested in Indian food?"

A German's Praise for India

"Interest in Indian food came later," the younger one replied. "It was interest in Indian music that came first. I am a Ravi Shankar fan. The sitar draws out the best in me. You don't know the wonderful things your country is doing for people like me."

I could feel that I was getting goose bumps. I tried to be as objective as I could while answering his curious questions about India. My memory jogged back a few years.

In late 2001, I was having food at a Rio de Janeiro restaurant. A total stranger, sitting at a few tables away, came up to me and handed me a napkin, with "Ravi Shankar, Good" scribbled on it. Though he spoke only a few words of English, he, his girlfriend and I spent the rest of the evening happily together, thanks to Ravi Shankar.

When I narrated that experience to the two Germans, the younger one said, "I can't wait to visit your country, man."

He and his friend were born and brought up at Nuremberg. No sooner had he uttered "Nuremberg" than he added, "I know what is going through your mind. I hope you won't hold it against us."

"Are you referring to the Nuremberg trials and the crimes committed by the Nazis that necessitated the trials?" I asked. "I am not that stupid. Nobody should condemn the entire people of a country for what a tyrant did while in power six decades ago. As long as you are not part of that tiny minority in the country that still admires Hitler, nobody will have any problem with you."

"But many in my country," he said, "especially those my age, still have some kind of guilt feeling."

I could sense a touch of guilt in the two young men too. "That's but natural," I told them, hoping to help them get rid of that hang-up. "That's the case with decent human beings in most countries. They can't help feeling responsible for the atrocities committed in the past by some of their countrymen. They carry the baggage all their lives. But in your case, being natives of Nuremberg should make you proud. The historic trials that sent Nazi criminals to the gallows and jails took place in your hometown. You have every reason to be proud, not ashamed, of being Nurembergers."

Looking at my watch, I added, "I had a long day. It started in the Baltic State of Latvia early this morning. I must try and get some sleep."

As I was getting ready to leave, both of them stood up and hugged me. "We thank you for the wonderful evening," the older one said.

"The feeling is mutual," I told them. "We'll continue our conversation tomorrow."

I said to myself, while taking leave of them, "Whoever thought that a country that produced adorable people like these two could also produce a tyrant like Hitler!"

20

How I Celebrated the 65ᵗʰ Anniversary of Warsaw Uprising Against Nazis

August 1, 2009 – Saturday

I was planning on sleeping longer this morning. But something that sounded like the shouting of slogans woke me up. When I looked out the third-floor window of the hostel, I saw a procession, about 100-strong, heading toward I didn't know where. But I did know that it had something to do with Polish politics. Most of those in the procession were carrying the Polish national flag.

I had a quick shower and went down to the reception desk to find out what it was about.

"Oh, they are celebrating the sixty-fifth anniversary of the Warsaw Uprising," the lady at the desk said. "There will be a special ceremony at the Warsaw Uprising Memorial in Krasinski Square, at five p.m. It's an annual event held in memory of those killed in the uprising, which broke out exactly at five p.m., on August 1, 1944. Today, there will be various kinds of commemorative activities all over the city. Don't be alarmed if you hear sirens blaring throughout the city at the stroke of five."

I thanked the receptionist for the information. "The Warsaw Uprising Memorial in Krasinski Square will be one of the places I visit today," I told her and went into the kitchen for a quick breakfast.

I broached the topic of the Warsaw Uprising with others at my breakfast table, hoping that some of them would be interested in joining me on my trip to Krasinski Square. None of them was, and I decided to go all by myself.

Everything I had read about the Warsaw Uprising, especially the events that led to it, came to mind the moment I stepped out of the hostel.

Germany invaded Poland on September 1, 1939, marking the beginning of World War II. Throughout the war, Warsaw, and much of Poland, was under Nazi occupation. Though some kind of insurgent activities had been going on from the very beginning of the occupation, they remained subdued and underground. The first-ever open rebellion, later known as the Warsaw Uprising, occurred on August 1, 1944, when 23,000 poorly armed soldiers of the Polish Home Army attacked Nazi positions in Warsaw. The first shot was fired in Krasinski Square. When other underground units and Warsaw citizens joined the uprising, the insurgents' ranks swelled to 50,000. But still, they were no match for the 1.5 million German troops who had spread across Poland.

The uprising was timed to coincide with the promised advance of Soviet troops toward the eastern suburbs of Warsaw. It was hoped that the Soviet advance would force the Germans to retreat. But the Soviet Red Army, on orders from dictator Josef Stalin, stood by on the east bank of the Vistula River, while the Germans crushed the uprising.

Stalin also thwarted British and American efforts to airlift supplies to the insurgents by refusing permission for their planes to refuel at airfields under the Red Army's control. His reasoning was that the uprising was an irresponsible act that would set back the Allies' war efforts. The actual reason, it came to light later, was Stalin's fear that a victory for the insurgents would lay the foundation for an independent postwar Poland, which in turn would frustrate his grandiose plan to bring all of Eastern Europe under Soviet domination.

It was commendable that, with little help from outside, the insurgents put up a brave fight for 63 days. When German troops, who were heavily armed and who vastly outnumbered the Polish Home Army, turned Warsaw into an inferno, the commander of the Home Army, Gen. Tadeusz "Bor" Komorowski, was left with no option but to surrender. By then, he had lost 15,000 of his men. The city as a whole had lost a quarter of its one-million population. On the German side, about 25,000 were reportedly killed, wounded or missing in action.

After the uprising was crushed, the Germans ordered the surviving residents of Warsaw to leave the city and then looted and destroyed what was left of it. About 85 percent of the city, including all of its Old Town area, the area that had been the historic center of Warsaw since the 13th century, was reduced to pebbles. Those who had refused to leave the city and were still alive were taken prisoner. Many of them were sent to Nazi concentration camps.

Germany Repairs Relations with Poland

Germany, after its reunification in 1990, has taken various steps toward making amends for the Nazi atrocities and repairing its strained relations with Poland. One important step was the touching gesture made at the Warsaw Uprising Memorial, on August 1, 2004, by Gerhard Schroeder, the Chancellor of Germany at the time. It was the 60th anniversary of the uprising and Schroeder, Chancellor of Germany from 1998 to 2005, was the chief guest at the annual commemoration ceremony held at the memorial. At the ceremony, according to an Associated Press report, he bowed on the steps of the memorial and said, "Today we bow in shame in the face of the Nazi troops' crimes. At this place of Polish pride and German shame, we hope for reconciliation and peace."

On August 1, 2009, the 65th anniversary of the uprising, I stood on the same steps that Mr. Schroeder did five years earlier and bowed my head. While Schroeder bowed his head in shame, I did it out of respect for all the Poles who sacrificed their lives in their fight against the Nazis.

The bouquets and wreaths of flowers, placed on the steps by those who had come and paid their respects before me, were still lying there. Hundreds of candles lighted by them were still burning in urns of various sizes. The scene struck me as a reassurance that the world would never forget what the Nazis had done to Poland during their occupation and during their ruthless suppression of the uprising in Warsaw.

I headed for the Old Town area of the city, which was just a ten-minute walk from where I was. While wandering in the area, I had to keep reminding myself that what I was seeing was a re-created version of the old Old Town that I had read, and heard a lot, about. Looking at the monuments, buildings and streets – the City Walls; the Cathedral of St John; the churches dedicated to Our Lady, St. James and the Holy Trinity; the Royal Castle which is now a museum; the Market Square where regular fairs and festivals used to be held; and so on – I was amazed that they all looked exactly like how they have been described in history books.

The recreation of Old Town, done between 1945 and 1966, has been so thorough and meticulous that the UNESCO describes it as "an exceptional example of the comprehensive reconstruction of a city that had been deliberately and totally destroyed." Poland has earned plaudits from around the world for this marvelous feat. In 1980, the UNESCO added the Warsaw Old Town to its list of World Heritage Sites.

Warsaw Ghetto Uprising

My next destination was another memorial, to another Warsaw uprising against the Nazis. Unlike the 1944 uprising in which Poles of all religious persuasions participated – Poland was, and still is, 90 percent Catholic – this one was organized exclusively by Jews living in the ghetto of Warsaw. It stood out in one more respect: While the 1944 uprising was initiated by members of Poland's Home Army who had some weapons and weapons training, this one was done by the residents of ghetto who had neither. (A few weapons were smuggled in by them later.) What has gone down in history as the Warsaw Ghetto Uprising began on April 19, 1943 and ended on May 16, 1943. It ended when the Nazis blew up the Great Synagogue of Warsaw.

There had been underground resistance movements among Jews living in various Eastern European countries, ever since those countries came under Nazi occupation. There had also been uprisings in some of the 100 ghettos in which they lived. Notable among them were the uprisings in the ghettos of Poland, Lithuania, Byelorussia (now Belarus), and the Ukraine. They occurred between 1941 and 1943. The largest, and the most memorable, was the Warsaw Ghetto Uprising of 1943.

Massive deportations of Jews from the Warsaw ghetto to the concentration and extermination camps set up by the Nazis at Treblinka, 50 miles away, began on July 22, 1942. More than 250,000 were deported over the following two months. Reports of mass murder taking place at the Treblinka camp enraged those who were still living in the Warsaw ghetto. When it became clear that the same fate was going to befall them too, a small group of them decided to fight back.

The leadership role in this was played by a 23-year-old Jew, by the name of Mordechai Anielewicz. He hurriedly put together an organization called *Żydowska Organizacja Bojowa* (the Jewish Combat Organization) or ŻOB. On April 19, 1943, the German troops and police entered the ghetto and ordered the residents to assemble outside, for shipment to Treblinka. Some of them obeyed, but the vast majority, as was instructed by the ŻOB, defied the order. About 750 members of the ŻOB, under the leadership of Mr. Anielewicz, launched an attack on the Germans. That was the beginning of the Warsaw Ghetto Uprising.

It is a testament to the character of the Jewish fighters that they chose to fight and die rather than allow themselves to be rounded up for eventual extermination. Remarkably, they managed to fight the vastly outnumbered and out-equipped

Nazis for almost a month. On May 16, 1943, the day the Nazis blew up the Great Synagogue of Warsaw, the surviving members of the ŻOB decided to stop fighting. Once the symbol of their very being was destroyed, the Jews lost the will to fight. It is said that the destruction of the synagogue, which was considered "a jewel of 19th-century architecture," was done on special orders from Hitler himself.

The Nazis shot and killed 7,000 of the more than 56,000 surviving ghetto residents. The rest were sent to Treblinka. After that, the whole Warsaw ghetto was razed to the ground.

All those chilling historical facts flashed through my mind as I approached the monument to the Warsaw Ghetto Uprising. From a distance, the monument, unveiled on April 19, 1948, looked nothing more than a wall. But as I came closer, it became clear to me that it was a fitting tribute to the brave Jews who valiantly stood up to the Nazis and courted deaths.

On the 36-foot-tall wall are figures in relief and cast in bronze, of men, women and children, armed with guns and Molotov cocktails. The figure of Mordechai Anielewicz, the young man who led the uprising, is very prominent. The wall of the monument is rich in symbolism. According to the late Nathan Rapoport, the sculptor whose brainchild the whole monument is, the wall represents the walls of the Warsaw ghetto as well as the "Wailing Wall" of Jerusalem, one of Judaism's holiest sites.

A few yards away from the monument, construction activities were going on for a museum* that would preserve the history of the entire Polish Jewry, especially their triumphs and tribulations before the Holocaust. Before World War II and the Holocaust,

---

*To get slightly ahead of the story, the museum, called the Museum of the History of Polish Jews and funded largely by Polish taxpayers, was opened on April 19, 2013, coinciding with the 70th anniversary of the Warsaw Ghetto Uprising. The Associated Press reported on the eve of the museum's opening that, apart from preserving the history of Poland's Jews, it also "dares to confront Poles with a truth many would once have strongly denied: that this country has had its own dark chapters of anti-Semitism."

Poland had 3.3 million Jews, making them the largest per capita Jewish population in any European country at the time.

I stood in silence before the monument and paid my respects to all the Jewish victims of Nazi atrocities – all those killed during the ghetto uprising and murdered at the Treblinka concentration camp. The number is between 870,000 and 925,000, according to the *Holocaust Encyclopedia*.

Celebrations on Nowy Swiat Street

On my way back to the hostel, as the bus passed by Nowy Swiat, a thoroughfare in Warsaw, I noticed that it was closed to traffic. There were crowds milling around. They too were celebrating the 65th anniversary of the Warsaw Uprising. I got off the bus and joined the celebrations.

Nowy Swiat, which means the new world, has a storied past. It was the street where the nobles in the country had their manors and palaces.

The Nazis pummeled them and all other buildings on the street, in retaliation for the uprising. Post-World War II Communist rulers of Poland, to their credit, gave top priority to reconstructing all important buildings and restoring Nowy Swiat Street to its old grandeur – to the extent possible. Today, the street is known for its recreation centers, shops, boutiques, restaurants, and bars.

By the time I reached there, the celebrations were winding down. A band was playing on a temporary stage set up on one side of the street. A banner hung across the stage had this written in bold letters: "rockowo – motocyklowo." I took it to be the name of the band.

As I approached the stage, the band was playing a Polish song. It was so frustrating that I understood only two words – "Polaski Poland" – from the song. To my surprise and delight, however, the next song, which was the finale of the event, was in English. It ended thus:

They are beautiful.
You look beautiful.
Wonderful.

I walked toward the hostel, saying to myself, "My experience in Warsaw, on the 65th anniversary of the Warsaw Uprising, turned out to be wonderful too."

21

Stalin's Gift to Polish People or Elephant in Lacy Underwear?

August 2, 2009 – Sunday

This was my last day in Warsaw. I made it a point to remind myself of that, as I got up in the morning. More importantly, I reminded myself that there were a few more places I was keen on visiting before saying farewell to the city. The uppermost on the list of those places was the Palace of Science and Culture. Most travel brochures say that it was Stalin's precious gift to the Polish people.

Being a Sunday, the streets were nearly empty. At the bus-stop outside the hostel, there was only one person waiting for the bus – a young woman, 20-something, very pretty and pleasant-looking. I asked her which bus would take me to "the building that is supposed to be Stalin's gift to the Polish people."

I took the liberty of being sarcastic about Stalin, because most young Poles I had talked with until then were bitter about their country's Communist past. The young woman gave me a smile and said, "I know which building you are talking about. But I am new to this place. Instead of guessing which bus takes you there, I will check with the driver of the first bus that arrives and get you the correct information."

She said she was from "a small town, about one hundred

kilometers away." She was a doctoral student in economics. She had been in Warsaw only a month. "I am working on my dissertation," she said. "I came here to continue my research. Warsaw being the capital of the country, I am hoping to find here a lot of material on my subject. My hometown doesn't have any good library. My college is not of much help either." So she decided to come to Warsaw "to knock at every door, seeking help. It has been a frustrating experience," she said.

"What is your dissertation on?" I asked.

"It's on the growth of venture capitalism in Poland."

"That's a fairly new topic for dissertation even in an advanced capitalist country," I told her. "You may have to put up with a lot of frustration at this stage. But once you complete your doctorate, you will be a pioneer in your field. You won't find many who have specialized in venture capitalism in all of Poland. Or in any country that came out of communism in the recent past, for that matter. Communism, as your parents knew it, will never come back here. So you have a wonderful future. I have a Ph.D. in political science. My tribe is a dime a dozen in any country. You will be very much in demand here once you complete your studies."

"I hope you are right," she said. "Thank you for those encouraging words." Looking at the bus that was approaching, she said, "I think this is the bus you should be taking. Let me confirm it."

When the bus stopped, she said something to the driver, in Polish. Then she turned to me and said, "Yes, this is your bus." She shook hands with me and added, "Enjoy your say in Warsaw."

"Good luck with your research," I told her. "I know dissertation is a lonely and boring enterprise. But never give up."

The driver shouted something in Polish, which I took to mean: "Cut that crap and get in." I rushed in.

In a few minutes, I was at the Palace of Culture and Science or *Palac Kultury i Nauki*, as Poles call it. It was built by 7,000 workers, evenly divided between Soviets and Poles. Though it was supposed to be Stalin's gift to the Polish people, he did not live to see the formal handing over of the gift. Its construction, which began on May 1, 1951, was completed only on July 22, 1955. Stalin died on March 5, 1953.

Russian Wedding Cake

Not all Poles were enamored of the gift, though. To many, it was a symbol of Poland's unsavory past, a past dominated by the Soviet Union and governed by the communist ideology. Its architectural design resembles Soviet skyscrapers of that period. Many others hated it because it "destroyed the esthetic balance of the old city and imposed dissonance with other buildings." They referred to it in pejorative terms like "elephant in lacy underwear," "Russian wedding cake," "Stalin's syringe," and so on. From a distance, the 778-foot-tall structure, with a spire on top, does look like a syringe.

However, the critics began to recognize its importance, as tourists began to flock to the place in large numbers and it became a revenue-earner for the country.

Over 550 ornamental sculptures adorn the building. It has a conference hall that can seat 3,000 people. In all, it has 3,288 rooms, which are used to host various events – fairs, exhibitions, art shows, and the likes.

One musical event, which the staffs of the place are not tired of talking about even now, is the Rolling Stones' 1967 concert. It was an epochal event because it was the first-ever performance behind the Iron Curtain by a famous Western rock band. Since then, other famous Western musicians – Leonard Cohen, Marlene Dietrich, Luciano Pavarotti, Eric Clapton and Tori Amos, to name a few – have performed here. But their performances did not have the historic significance, which the one by the Rolling Stones had.

I visited the place for the same reason that most tourists do: to get a panoramic view of all of Warsaw which its 30th-floor viewing platform provides.

The view was panoramic, all right. But it did raise an important question in my mind: What would Stalin think of all the skyscrapers that have come up around the building that is supposed to be an example of "Socialist Realist [socrealist] architecture"? Most of them, if anything, proclaim to the world how far Poland has come from its socialist past. The logos of capitalist multinational corporations – Marriott Hotel, ORCO Tower, InterContinental Warsaw, Bank Austria Creditanstalt, Peugeot, etc. – that blazon the skyline could make Stalin turn in his grave.

According to the brochure I had picked up at the entrance to the building, there was an exhibition going on, on the sixth floor. I stopped by to take a look. The only exhibits on display were electronic games; quizzes programmed into some toy-like devices, by playing which one could find out one's health condition; and items of that nature. Most of them were of interest only to teenagers.

I had hoped to see in the building, given as a gift to the Polish people in the name of Stalin, something that would perpetuate his memory. There was none. Though disappointed, I was careful not to show it.

I even tried to be gracious about the late Soviet dictator's 'generosity.' At the end of my visit, while in the elevator going down, I remarked, to no one in particular: "After all, Stalin did something good for the Polish people."

A middle-aged woman standing nearby gave me a contemptuous look and said, "What do you mean?"

"This wonderful building," I replied.

"This is the only good thing he did for us." She followed it with a gesture of wiping sweat from the forehead with her index finger. Most people in the elevator burst out laughing.

The gesture about summed up the attitude of many Poles I met in Warsaw toward Stalin, and communism in general.

After coming out of the building, I spent some time walking on Jerusalem Avenue – *Aleje Jerozolimskie,* in Polish. The avenue has a storied past. As its name suggests, it has a Jewish connection too. In 1774, a Jewish settlement was established in the city, in what is today's Zawiszy Square, and the road that led to the settlement was called Jerusalem Road. Though the then-Warsaw authorities, fearing competition in trade, demolished the settlement a year later, the name stuck. And it has survived to this day.

A 50-foot 'palm tree' that stands in the de Gaulle Roundabout of Jerusalem Avenue is also a reminder of its Jewish connection. Though it looks like a verdant palm tree, it is actually made of steel, plastic and other materials. It is a work of art contributed by the London-based Polish artist Joanna Rajkowska. She titled her artwork "Greetings from Jerusalem Avenue" and made it look like the palm trees one sees in Israeli cities – to emphasize, again, the avenue's Jewish connection.

I spent a few minutes around Constitution Square (*Plac Konstytucji*). The square, together with the Palace of Culture and Science, represents the "socrealist" architecture. "Socrealist" was the label the Communists proudly attached to the architecture that evolved in Warsaw in the 1949-1956 period. The square gets its name not from Poland's cherished 1791 constitution, but from the Stalinist constitution the country adopted on July 22, 1951 or, more appropriately, the constitution Stalin imposed on Poland on that day.

Because it was my last day in Warsaw, I had some packing to do. So I decided to head back to my hostel. I asked a woman who was passing by whether I was anywhere near Nowy Swiat. Most people in Warsaw knew this famous street, and I knew my way to the hostel from there.

"Yes, it's only walking distance," the woman said, adding, "I am going in that direction." I surmised from her reply that she wouldn't mind my walking with her.

We walked together, talking about various things. A Polish postal employee, she knew her country's history well. When we reached a spot where a few people were seen respectfully looking at some flowers and burning candles, I asked her what it was about.

It was a makeshift memorial, she said, set up by the residents of the neighborhood to honor those killed in that neighborhood during the Warsaw Uprising. "During the 63-day uprising," she added, "sporadic fighting broke out in various parts of the city. If you go around the city, you will see makeshift memorials like this one in many more places."

The flowers, placed there the day before in observance of the uprising's 65th anniversary, had already begun to wilt. But the candles were still burning. So was the patriotic spirit in the lady who was with me. She was very emotional when she referred to the uprising and to her compatriots whom the Nazis massacred during the uprising. She was silent the next few minutes. And I was careful not to disturb it.

She broke her silence when we reached Nowy Swiat. "This is the street you asked me about," she said.

"How about a coffee?" I asked her.

"No. I have to rush home. My two little daughters are waiting for me. Thank you. Send me an email when you reach home."

We exchanged our email addresses. I shook hands with her and said, "I enjoyed talking and walking with you. Thank you."

Buddha Indian Restaurant

Nowy Swiat was bustling with Sunday-evening crowds. I was entering the street at the opposite end from where I had entered it the previous day. A signboard that was staring at me from one side of the street read: "Buddha Indian restaurant."

In the three days I had been in Warsaw I had seen only one other business establishment that appeared Indian-owned. It turned out to be Indian-owned only in appearance. It was actually owned by a Polish woman. She called it "India Shop" because it sold Indian materials. The materials – Indian clothes, antiques and artifacts – were attractively displayed on the windows of her shop. The woman, 60-something, who owned it was attractive too – another reason why I visited the store.

After taking a quick look at all the items in the store, I had asked her, "Does your fascination for Indian materials come from your visits to India?"

She had never been to India, she said. "All the items you see here are genuinely Indian, though," she added. "I imported them from trustworthy Indian parties. I like India. But my interest in these Indian goods is purely commercial."

"I admire your candor," I said. While leaving the store, I wished her "much success."

That happened the day I arrived in Warsaw. The incident came back to mind as I walked toward the Buddha Indian Restaurant. I went in – more to find out whether the owner of this place also had a story similar to that of the Polish owner of the "India Shop" than to eat.

No, the restaurant was 100 percent Indian-owned. It is owned by Sunil from Mumbai. He said he had been living in Warsaw for 20 years. Before switching to restaurant business, he was importing and exporting textiles. "I started this restaurant only last year," he told me.

The restaurant was packed with customers. The food was genuinely Indian, prepared by an Indian chef. Sunil introduced the chef to me, "Prakash from Chennai." And then he added, "Maybe you two speak the same language."

"No," I said, "but you are close. I am from the neighboring state of Kerala and I understand Tamil, Prakash's mother tongue."

"I understand Malayalam too," Prakash said, referring to the language of Kerala, which is my mother tongue.

An Admirer of Lech Walesa

Sunil got very excited while answering my questions about his 20 years' experience in Poland. More so, when he talked about the revolutionary changes that occurred in the country during those 20 years. He said that he was a proud witness to Poland's transition from a Soviet satellite to an independent, non-Communist country. His face lit up when he talked about

Lech Walesa who, through the Solidarity movement he had co-founded in 1980, brought about that transition.

Solidarity was the first-ever non-Communist trade union movement in the entire Communist Bloc. The movement was largely instrumental in the collapse of communism in Poland and the success of the movement was largely attributable to Lech Walesa. As Timothy Garton Ash wrote in his article on Walesa, in the April 13, 1988, issue of *TIME* magazine, "It is one of history's great ironies that the nearest thing we have ever seen to a genuine workers' revolution was directed against a so-called workers' state… . Walesa's contribution to the end of communism in Europe, and hence the end of the cold war, stands beside those of his fellow Pole, Pope John Paul II…."

Though by the time I was in Poland, Mr. Walesa's popularity had dimmed considerably, and many allegations had been swirling around him, Sunil still remained an ardent admirer of him. His reasoning was: "Whatever success I have had in this country is because of the collapse of communism and that collapse occurred because of Lech Walesa."

"I fully agree with you on that," I told him. "I am in a bit of a hurry. Otherwise, I would have continued talking with you. I wish you all the best."

"Why don't you have dinner here?" he said. "Something for memory."

"I have a few things to take care of before dinner," I said. "You have already made a valuable addition to my memorable experiences in Warsaw."

"But you must have something," he insisted. I settled for a cup of tea.

I walked toward my hostel, feeling good about how my last day in Warsaw began and ended. The few places I visited and the people I met made the day memorable.

22

From Dubcek to Havel: A Mental Journey through Czech History

August 3, 2009 – Monday

I was on my way to Prague, the capital of the Czech Republic. Relaxing on the plane, half asleep, I took a mental tour of that part of Czechoslovak history that had fascinated me when I was a journalism student in Bombay (now Mumbai).

At that time, the Czech Republic and Slovakia were the integral parts of one federation called Czechoslovakia. Before World War II, as now, they were two separate political entities. Czechoslovakia came into being when, in the postwar realignment of the erstwhile Nazi-controlled countries, Slovakia merged with the Czech Republic. The latest split occurred on January 1, 1993.

The first time I got interested in Czechoslovakia's politics and its people was when a charismatic new leader arrived on the county's political scene and initiated a series of reforms. The new leader was Alexander Dubcek, who became first secretary of the Czechoslovak Communist Party on January 5, 1968. I was one of those who were fascinated by the political reforms he initiated in Czechoslovakia soon after he entered office. Until then, such reforms were unheard of in a Soviet-Bloc country. Czechoslovakia had been part of the Soviet Bloc since the end of World War II.

The Prague Spring

Within weeks of taking office, Dubcek started his move toward the "widest possible democratization" of his country and establishment of "a free, modern, and profoundly humane society." He relaxed the Communist Party's control over the media and started rehabilitating the victims of the Stalinist-era political purges. He also revised the country's constitution to guarantee civil rights and liberties to its citizens. The sudden, bold changes came to be called the Prague Spring. The architect of the change did not make any such claim, though. What he was aiming at, he repeatedly said, was "socialism with a human face."

The democratic reforms Mr. Dubcek initiated won him admirers around the world. The people of Czechoslovakia overwhelmingly supported the reforms. In fact, they started demanding speedier democratic transformation. But the sudden change upset hard-line Communists in the country and their Soviet overlords. To quote from an obituary of Dubcek (he died on November 7, 1992) that appeared in the November 9, 1992, issue of *The New York Times,* "nothing remotely resembling such independence had existed in Eastern Europe since the unsuccessful Hungarian uprising of 1956, which also had been crushed by Soviet troops."

Hard-line Communists called the reforms counterrevolutionary. The Soviet Union saw in them a threat to the Warsaw Pact, of which Czechoslovakia was a member. On August 21, 1968, Soviet troops, joined by troops from four other Warsaw Pact countries – East Germany, Poland, Hungary and Bulgaria – invaded Czechoslovakia.

In Bombay, among us journalism students, Alexander Dubcek had become a hero. The Prague Spring and the Soviet invasion of Czechoslovakia became topics of animated conversation among us. I remember reading accounts of unarmed students and workers confronting Soviet tanks and soldiers with flowers and placards, pleading with them to go home. But to no avail.

Within a few days, according to one report, 20 Czechoslovaks were killed and more than 300 wounded.

Several members of the government, including Prime Minister Dubcek, were arrested. The Soviets put hard-line Communists back in power. All the new political, social and economic measures Dubcek had introduced were revoked. In April 1969, he was removed as leader of the Czechoslovak Communist Party and replaced with Gustav Husak.

But the Communists who came to power with the blessings of the Soviet Union could not squelch forever the passion for political change that Dubcek reforms had kindled. In less than a decade after the suppression of the Prague Spring, the new leaders found their authority challenged. On January 1, 1977, more than 250 human rights activists signed and released a document criticizing the government for its failure to meet its human rights obligations. The document was called "Charter 77." The releasing of the document marked the beginning of Eastern Europe's oldest human-rights movement.

At the forefront of the movement was the country's well-known playwright Vaclav Havel, who was also a co-author of "Charter 77." As was expected, the signers of the document were harassed by police. Most of them lost their jobs and a few dozen were sent to jail. Mr. Havel spent five years in jail. Some of the activists went into exile.

The Velvet Revolution

Charter 77 was the precursor of the famous nonviolent political movement in Czechoslovakia, known as the Velvet Revolution. As we all know, it was the Velvet Revolution that ended the Communist Party's rule in the country. In the beginning, the revolution took the form of public protests and demonstrations.

Notable among them were the mass demonstrations of August 1988, organized to mark the anniversary of the 1968 Soviet invasion that crushed the Prague Spring. Over a year later, in November 1989, a series of rallies were held in major cities of the country, protesting against the government's human rights violations. Unable to turn back the strong tide, the government collapsed. The chief architect of the Velvet Revolution was Vaclav Havel.

A transition government was formed in December 1989, with Marian Calfa as prime minister and Vaclav Havel as president. At the height of the revolution, Dubcek re-emerged as a national leader. He was unanimously elected chairman of the Federal Assembly. The country was renamed Czech and Slovak Federative Republic.

The elections held in 1990 – the first free elections since 1946 – brought into office a coalition government involving all major parties, with the exception of the Communist Party of Czechoslovakia. Havel retained his presidency.

Czechoslovakia Breaks Up

In 1992, negotiations on the new federal constitution deadlocked over the issue of autonomy for Slovakia. Over President Havel's objections and despite a lack of popular enthusiasm for it, an agreement was reached to dissolve Czechoslovakia into its two separate political entities. On July 20, 1992, Havel tendered his resignation, saying that he would not preside over the country's breakup. On January 1, 1993, Czechoslovakia formally split into two independent states – the Czech Republic and Slovakia.

Dubcek, though a native of Slovakia, was opposed to the split. He was spared the pain and embarrassment of witnessing it, because he had died two months before the split, at the age of 70.

Havel could not stay away from politics for too long. He stood for election in the newly created Czech Republic and became its first president. Unlike in the erstwhile Czechoslovakia, the president of the Czech Republic was the country's chief executive only nominally. The real power was vested in the prime minister. However, the constitutional limitations on presidential powers notwithstanding, Havel as a person commanded a great deal of moral authority. Thanks to that authority, he was able to keep the Communist Party of the country at bay throughout his tenure as president. In 1998, he was re-elected. His second term ended on February 2, 2003.

My brief mental journey through the phase of Czechoslovakia's political history that started with the Dubcek era came to an abrupt end when an announcement came from the captain of the plane that we had started descending toward the Ruzyně International Airport, Prague.

(To get slightly ahead of the story, Vaclav Havel died on December 18, 2011, and the airport was renamed the Václav Havel International Airport, on October 5, 2012. When Havel died, he was more popular abroad than at home. At home, some of his initiatives and pronouncements had become controversial. But his firm stand against communism, especially the Stalinist variant of it, and the contribution he had made in transforming Czechoslovakia into a democratic polity and a free-market economy had won him admirers all over the world. As U.S. President Barack Obama said in the condolence message sent on his death, Vaclav Havel's "peaceful resistance shook the foundations of an empire, exposed the emptiness of a repressive ideology, and proved that moral leadership is more powerful than any weapon.")

A Quiz on Geography for Two Russian Girls

It was well past noon by the time I checked into my hotel in Prague. It was a bright, sunny day. Though tired, I was impatient to get to the action center of the city. I headed for Prague's Old Town Square right away.

The square was filled with tourists of various nationalities. I heard more languages spoken there than I could recognize. Two girls, bubbly and noisy, were looking at an elegant building and

My Thirty-Day European Odyssey

saying something, in Russian. I asked them, in English, whether they knew what the building housed.

They didn't. "We are from St. Petersburg," one of them said.

"Are you students?"

"Yes," both of them replied. They were studying economics and had two more years left to complete their bachelor's degree.

"Which country are you from?" the bubblier of the two asked me.

I gave my stock reply to that question: "Take a guess. Hardly anyone has gone wrong."

After a few seconds' giggling, the other one said, "America?"

"How many Americans you have met look like me?" I said.

They continued to giggle.

"I can make you feel good, though," I added, "I live in America. But I am originally from a country that is geographically closer to yours. Guess a few countries that are geographically close to Russia."

They couldn't guess even one.

"OK," I tried to help them out, "let's start with Afghanistan. Which country is next to Afghanistan?"

Again, they couldn't name it.

Again, I helped them out, "Pakistan. I am sure you know which country is next to Pakistan."

I felt disappointed when they started staring at each other and giggling. I decided to give up quizzing them and said, "India." "Good luck with your studies," I said and bade them good-bye.

I couldn't help contrasting them with the two other undergraduate Russian students I had met a few days earlier, one on the train, on my way to the Moscow airport, and the other, at the Riga hostel. Compared with them, these two girls were dumb.

On a positive note, the contrast reaffirmed to me that I shouldn't generalize a whole country on the basis of my experience with one or two of its citizens.

23

Tour of Prague, a City of Magnificent Monuments

August 4, 2009 – Tuesday

Prague is one of the few cities in Europe that came out of World War II almost intact. The city, with its narrow streets and cobbled passages, reminds one of an older, lost Europe. It has three sections: the Old Town, the Lesser Town and the New Town – *Staré Mesto, Mala Strana* and *Nové Mesto*, respectively, in the Czech language. It has been a place of great architectural and cultural influence since the Middle Ages. Its magnificent monuments, churches and palaces, built mostly in the 14th century by the Holy Roman Emperor, Charles IV, bear evidence to that fact.

The conducted tour of the city, which I was booked on, would start from Old Town Square at 10 a.m. I had been told to join the rest of the tour group under the famous Astronomical Clock in the square. "Be there a few minutes earlier," the man who sold me the tour ticket had said. "You don't want to miss the clock's fascinating mechanical performance that happens every hour, on the hour."

I would be the last person to miss it, because I had heard a lot about this clock even before.

At the stroke of every hour, two windows open up on the

My Thirty-Day European Odyssey

sides of the clock to reveal 12 apostles greeting the city. Also seen on the sides, suddenly animated on the hour, are a skeleton ringing a bell, a Turk shaking his head, a miser with a bag containing money, and Vanity looking in a mirror. The whole performance ends with the crowing of a golden rooster and the ringing of a huge bell atop the tower. Legend has it that the ghosts and devils flee the city at the first cock-crow in the morning.

One can tell from the clock dial what day it is and its position in the week, month and year. The clock also tracks Central European, Babylonian and Sidereal times. All this made the clock one of the wonders of the world in the Middle Ages. Since it was built in 1410, it has been attracting tourists in droves – except during the "decades of slumber under first the Nazis and then the Communists and, centuries before that, the Habsburgs," as the *National Geographic* puts it. Now, "Prague drips with history," the magazine adds, "but it's hardly a museum piece. The booming tourist industry has fed a revival of the city's arts and museums, and made its hotels and restaurants the envy of Central Europe."

After watching the wonders performed by the Astronomical Clock, our tour group moved on to the next stop: the Museum of Medieval Torture Instruments. The three floors of the museum are packed with all kinds of torture instruments, with detailed explanations on their use given in eight languages. Some objects needed little explanation, though. Anyone could tell, for example, that "The Break Knee" instrument was used to break the knees of criminals, a mode of punishment in medieval times. Again, one doesn't need any explanatory note to figure out the kind of pain the victims suffered when forced to sit naked on "The Interrogation Seat," a chair with spikes on it, until they collapsed or expired. The same goes for several other torture instruments displayed in the museum.

The questions raised by some of the visitors to the museum on the authenticity of some exhibits are very pertinent. Referring to the famous "Iron Maiden," also known as "the

Virgin of Nuremberg," which is a kind of stone coffin lined with strategically placed spikes that would pierce the person locked inside, this is what a visitor has written: "Interestingly, there is no documented use of the Iron Maiden before 1793, so it was really not a medieval instrument at all... . There are no documented uses of the Iron Maiden in the Czech Lands. You also get no real idea how many of the other implements were used in the Czech Lands."

After spending a little over half an hour in the museum, I came away mulling over the view expressed by another visitor: "Is this gruesome collection of pain-inducing paraphernalia educational, entertaining or just a tourist rip-off?" The fact that there are a lot of commercial activities, aimed at tourists, on the ground floor of the museum makes the question very relevant.

Charles Bridge

Next, we took a walk on the famous Charles Bridge (*Karluv most*, in the Czech language). Built in the 14th century and named for King Charles IV who ordered its construction, the 1,673-foot-long bridge has been the main pedestrian route across the Vltava River, connecting the Old Town and the Lesser Town. However, it is more than just a bridge used by pedestrians. It became a piece of art between 1600 and 1800, when "the Catholic desire for ornamentation resulted in 30 statues [of saints] being erected" on it.

Now there are 75 statues on the bridge, but most of them are copies of the original. The original ones, i.e., those that survived floods and other calamities, are now lying in the nearby Czech National Museum. Perhaps the oldest and the most interesting statue is that of John of Nepomuk, the patron saint of the Czech Republic. Story goes that he was thrown into the cold waters of the Vltava, in 1393, after "earning the ire" of King Wenceslas, Charles IV's son.

Though the Charles Bridge is a piece of art, we couldn't enjoy its beauty as much as we wanted to, because it was under renovation. Construction equipment and scaffoldings blocked the view of many interesting parts of the bridge. However, they did not block the beautiful view from the bridge of Prague and of the Vltava River flowing beneath the bridge.

Apart from tourists, the crowd on the bridge consisted of hawkers, portraitists and musicians. One writer described the musical scene on the bridge as "a 24/7 Mardi Gras celebration." We also saw artists sketching and painting portraits of passersby for a fee. The scene reminded me of Times Square in New York City in the tourist season. That, we were told, is another attraction of the Charles Bridge.

The Prague Castle

After crossing the bridge, we headed toward the Prague Castle, another tourist attraction in the Czech capital. Founded in 870, it was the seat of the kings of Bohemia for centuries and is said to be the largest medieval castle in Europe. Now, it is the official residence of the president of the Czech Republic.

The Prague Castle, or Hradcany Castle, is part of a vast complex covering an area of 18 acres, perched on a hill overlooking the Vltava River. The view of the city from the top of the hill was spectacular. This fairy-tale castle, reflecting the city's "Bohemian Baroque" architecture, has been renovated several times. It was transformed into a prestigious Gothic palace by Charles IV and remodeled again during the reign of Vladislav Jagellonský.

When we reached the castle's main gate, the hourly changing-of-the-guard ceremony was going on. We enjoyed watching the elaborate ceremony. Once inside the gate, we crossed a few courtyards and reached St. Vitus Cathedral, the real treasure within the castle which few tourists miss. An excellent example of Gothic architecture, it is the biggest and most important church in the country. It is now owned by the Czech government and contains the tombs of many Bohemian kings and Holy Roman Emperors.

Construction of the St. Vitus Cathedral began in 1344 but was not finished until 1929. After touring the inside, admiring the large stained glass windows, the small chapels that line the sides, the royal crypt downstairs, and the ornate St. Wenceslas Chapel, we reached the cathedral's Great South Tower, which holds the biggest bell in the Czech Republic. The bell was put up there in the 16th century.

When our guide said that one would get the best view of the city from the top of the tower, a few youngsters in our group started running up the steps. I was tempted to join them, but decided against it when the guide added that the tower was 90 meters tall and that there were 287 steps to climb. There were many more in our group who, like me, decided to save the energy for the rest of the tour. Instead of doing nothing until the energetic youngsters came back, we went around taking a second look at the frescoes and semi-precious stones of St. Wenceslas Chapel. The Bohemian Coronation Jewels are stored in the Crown Chamber of the chapel.

Next, we went inside the Royal Palace, where the main attraction is the Vratislav Hall, named for Prince Vratislav. The former coronation room renowned for its vaulted late-Gothic ceiling, it is still used for official state ceremonies. A short distance from the Royal Palace is St. George's Basilica, the interior of which has been described by some as "more solemn and stately than St. Vitus." Founded by Prince Vratislav in 920, St. George's Basilica is one of the few Romanesque buildings in Prague still standing. Within the basilica lie several tombs, notably those of Prince Vratislav, Boleslav II and St. Ludmila, the widow of the ninth-century ruler, Prince Borivoj.

Next, we were taken to the Golden Lane. Pointing to the "impossibly tiny dwellings" on the lane, the guide said, "You may be wondering whether anyone lived in them." Yes, they were the dwellings of the servants and marksmen of the Prague Castle, in the 16th century, he added. Pointing to dwelling number 22, he said that Franz Kafka, one of the most influential German-language writers of the 20th century, lived in it for a while.

Beyond the Golden Lane, we could see the tower of the Daliborka Prison. It got its name from Dalibor of Kozojedy, who was supposed to be the first prisoner there. He was imprisoned in 1498. Our guide told us an interesting story about Dalibor and his imprisonment.

He was a young knight who was sentenced to death for the 'crime' of sheltering some rebellious serfs. While waiting for his death in the dark, inhospitable prison dungeon, he learned to play the violin. People from the surrounding areas came to listen to his sad, touching music, and took pity on him. They brought him food and drink. He became so popular that the authorities feared to announce the date of his execution. One day, the violin did fall silent. The opera *Dalibor*, composed by Bedrich Smetana in the 19th century, is based on this story, which our guide relished narrating.

We continued walking until we came to the courtyard of the Lobkowicz Palace. The palace is a new museum displaying the noble family's valuable collections of paintings, sheet music, books, and weapons. The courtyard also houses a café and a toy museum, with its historic collection of classic dolls, wooden toys, trains, and games.

At this point, we were given the option of being on our own the rest of the evening or joining the guide on the tour bus to go back to Old Town Square where the tour began. I chose the latter option.

Visit to Jewish Quarter

On the way back, before reaching Old Town Square, the tour managed to squeeze in a visit to the Jewish Quarter. The history of the Jewish Quarter in Prague dates back to the 13th century, when a government-appointed body, called the Certification Board, ordered all Jews to vacate their homes in different parts of the city and settle only in one area. The area came to be called the Jewish Quarter or the Prague Jewish Ghetto.

Though the Jewish Quarter underwent a lot of structural

changes, most of the significant buildings from previous eras were saved. Among them are six synagogues, including the Old-New Synagogue and the Spanish Synagogue, the Jewish Town Hall and the Old Jewish Cemetery. The cemetery is said to be the most remarkable of its kind in Europe: For want of space, the dead were buried in layers, twelve-deep. The Old-New Synagogue is today the main house of prayer for Prague's 13,000-strong Jewish community. The Jewish Quarter is a living testimony to the history of Jews not only of Prague, but of the whole of Europe.

After the day-long tour, a fellow tourist, a Serb from Belgrade, and I were relaxing over a beer at one of the open-air cafes of Old Town Square. I started the conversation with questions about Yugoslavia under Marshal Tito and its later disintegration into independent countries, including his, Serbia. He did not know until then that the late Mr. Tito was one of the trio that started a new movement in world politics, called the Non-Alliance Movement, the other two being Jawaharlal Nehru of India and Gamal Abdel Nasser of Egypt. He thanked me "for the new piece of information."

Our conversation had just started getting animated, when I spotted in the packed crowd of the square a middle-aged woman and a teenage girl, both of whom looked very Indian. The woman was wearing a sari and had a vermilion spot on her forehead. I took the girl, in jeans and T-shirt, to be her daughter. Both the sari and the T-shirt were of the same color, blood-red. How red became their favorite color beat me. It couldn't be an expression of solidarity with the rulers of the country, for it had been long since the Czechs sent the Communists packing from positions of power. Whatever their political affiliation, I was keen on having a conversation with them. The reason? In the two days I had been in Prague, I had not seen one Indian.

"Look at those two women," I told my Serb acquaintance.

"They are the first Indians I have seen since I arrived here. Let me go and say hello to them. I'll be back in a couple of minutes."

"Go ahead," he said, "I will watch your stuff here."

I walked up to the two women and said, "Hello."

The girl looked at me and smiled. The woman completely ignored me. For the life of me, I didn't know why. Both of them walked away as though I didn't exist.

Disappointed, I came back to the table and guzzled the remaining beer in my glass.

"What happened?" the Serb asked. "I saw the woman ignoring you."

"Do I look like a rapist?" I asked him. "Even if I do, isn't the woman sensible enough to know that it can't happen in a crowded place like this?"

After a few seconds' silence, I added, "If she doesn't want a good son-in-law, it is her problem." The Serb laughed.

As both of us were tired, we decided to call it a day. We exchanged our phone numbers and email addresses, hugged each other, and said good-bye.

24

Why Terezin Concentration Camp Was Called the Paradise Ghetto

August 5, 2009 – Wednesday

The land on which Terezin now stands was once part of Bohemia. And Bohemia was a province in the Austrian Empire under the Habsburgs. Area-wise, Bohemia covered most of what is the Czech Republic today.

In 1780, Joseph II, the son of Austrian Empress Maria Theresa, ordered to build two fortresses, about 30 miles to the northwest of Prague. The purpose was to protect Austria from possible attacks from Prussia. A township developed within the fortresses, which the new emperor called Theresienstadt (*Terezin*, in the Czech language), after his mother. The mother had just died, making him the absolute ruler of Austria. His father, Francis I, had died in 1765.

When the fortresses ceased to have any military purpose, they were used as a prison. The most famous prisoner at the facility was Gavrilo Princip who had assassinated Archduke Franz Ferdinand of Austria, sparking World War I. Over two decades later, during World War II, the Nazis used it as a holding place for those whom they considered enemies – Jews, Gypsies, homosexuals, and all political opponents – and started rounding

My Thirty-Day European Odyssey

up. They were held there until the extermination camps further east were ready.

Over 7,000 residents of Terezin were evacuated to make room for the newly-arrived prisoners. Initially, they were put up in the barracks and, later, in civilian buildings commandeered for use as prison. Thus, by mid-1942, Terezín became the largest concentration camp in the Czech Lands. Unlike the other concentration camps, this one had no gas chambers, no mass machine-gun executions, and no medical testing rooms. It was a transit camp for prisoners on their way to Auschwitz and other extermination camps.

Among those held at Terezin were elderly, privileged, and famous Jews from Germany, Austria, the Czech Lands, and other areas in Europe that came under Nazi occupation. As the home of some of the most prominent artists, writers, scientists, jurists, diplomats, musicians, and scholars, the camp had a rich cultural life. Outstanding Jewish artists created drawings and paintings, some of them clandestine depictions of the ghetto's harsh reality. Writers and professors gave lectures; musicians gave concerts; and actors gave theater performances. The camp also maintained a lending library of 60,000 books. Even in the ghetto's inhuman conditions, the gifted among the inmates were able to express their creativity. Numerous poems and simple drawings of outstanding documentary value originated in this camp. While the concentration camps were generally referred to as ghettos, the one at Terezin was nicknamed the Paradise Ghetto.

The elderly and accomplished among the prisoners made sure that the children who passed through the camp – there were 15,000 of them at one time – continued to get the education they needed. They put the children through a rigorous daily routine of athletic activities and made them attend classes on various subjects. They taught the children how to paint pictures and write poetry. Despite such physical and mental exercises, not more than 1,100 children survived. (According to some estimates, the number is 150.)

Similar fate befell the grown-ups too. Although Terezin was designed as a transit camp, and not an extermination camp, overcrowding, filthy conditions, malnutrition and diseases claimed the lives of over 30,000 of the overall 150,000 prisoners interned there. In September 1942, there were 58,000 people living in an area once inhabited by 7,000 Czechs. Around 90,000 more were deported to Auschwitz and other extermination camps.

What really set Terezin apart from other concentration camps was its use by the Nazis as a propaganda tool. The absence of gas chambers and torture areas at this camp helped them in their propaganda. And the presence of a large number of artists among the prisoners enabled the Nazis to put together two plans to present Terezin as a model community full of cultural life.

In the first plan, they staged *Brundibár*, a children's opera composed in 1941 by Hans Krása, when a delegation from the International Committee of the Red Cross visited the camp. The children sang; the orchestra played; and the Red Cross was delighted. It gave Terezín a "clean bill of health." That within days of the event, almost all the children who performed in the opera were shipped to gas chambers is a different matter.

The second plan was far more deceptive. On June 23, 1944, three foreign observers, two of them from the Red Cross, came to Terezín to look into various charges leveled against it: that its inmates were subjected to cruel treatment; that the camp was badly overcrowded; and so on. The camp authorities did a good job of glossing over those charges. To deflect the charge of overcrowding, they shipped some 7,500 sick and elderly prisoners to Auschwitz, even before the observers arrived. Once they arrived, they were shown a documentary film featuring "happy" inmates playing football and cultivating gardens. The film, entitled *The Führer Gives a City to the Jews,* portrayed the Terezin camp as a "self-governing entity," a place of comfortable living.

The visitors were also entertained by the Terezín Orchestra, conducted by its founder, Karel Ancerl, who was among the Czech musicians interned at the camp. According to Anka Bergman, 96, a musician herself, who survived Terezin and narrowly escaped the gas chambers at Auschwitz, Ancerl's genius was exploited by the Nazis in furtherance of their sickening propaganda, "but he could not do otherwise." Duped by the well-planned and well-executed "beautification" of the camp, the observers left it with the impression that everything there was hunky-dory.

The propaganda and deception at Terezin went on until May 10, 1945, the day Soviet forces liberated it from the Nazis. (The Nazis had surrendered to the Allied Powers on May 7, 1945, ending the European-sector conflicts of World War II. The conflicts in the Pacific sector formally ended only on September 2, 1945.)

Visit to Terezin Memorial

Two years after the war ended, a memorial came up on the site of what was once the Terezin Concentration Camp. Opened on May 6, 1947, largely on the initiative of the newly-formed Czechoslovak government, the Terezin Memorial serves as a warning for future generations. I had the privilege of visiting it on August 5, 2009.

It has two main areas: the Large Fortress and the Small Fortress. The Large Fortress is essentially the town itself. The majority of the ghetto residents lived in the Large Fortress during the Nazi occupation. The Museum of the Ghetto, an important part of the Terezin Memorial and opened in 1991, is in this area. We were told that the exhibits in the museum were arranged with the assistance of former prisoners of the camp. The exhibits chronicle the rise of Nazism and daily life at the Terezin Ghetto.

After a few minutes' walk from the Large Fortress, we reached the Small Fortress – a smaller, more heavily fortified area where political prisoners were interned. It was also used as a torture zone. From 1940 to 1945, Czech and Moravian patriots and members of various resistance groups and organizations were sent here by the Prague Gestapo.

In five years, some 32,000 men and women passed through the gates of the Small Fortress. The conditions under which they lived steadily worsened. They were forced into slave labor. From 1943, executions were carried out without judicial process. More than 250 prisoners were shot dead. At the last execution, on May 2, 1945, 51 prisoners and one informer, lost their lives. Most of them belonged to the Předvoj youth movement.

As I entered the main gate of the Small Fortress, I got the same eerie feeling that I did when I entered the Dachau Concentration Camp Memorial a year earlier. At both places, the sign displayed above the main gate read the same: "ARBEIT MACHT FREI [Work Sets One Free]." For most of the inmates, that freedom came only with their deaths.

On the opposite side of the gate is the National Cemetery. It was created artificially after the camp's liberation. The stimulus for its creation came from former prisoners and the heirs of those who died. To create the cemetery, physical remains were exhumed from six mass graves in the ramparts of the Small Fortress. Among the remains exhumed were of those who had been put on the notorious death march toward the end of World War II. In all, the National Cemetery contains the remains of some 10,000 victims.

Chat with a Czech University Student

The tour of the Terezin Memorial was sold to us as "a sobering reminder of the atrocities" committed by the Nazis during World War II. The organizers of the tour did not let us down. I came out of the memorial asking the same question that I did when I came out of Dachau Concentration Camp Memorial: "How could human beings do such things to other human beings?" The question still lingered as I boarded the bus to get back to Prague. The pleasant conversation I had with the person sitting next to me helped me keep it off my mind.

My Thirty-Day European Odyssey

Anna was an undergraduate student in Prague, majoring in psychology. She was returning from a town beyond Terezin, after babysitting her niece, her sister's daughter. "I don't do it free," she said. "My sister pays me something. I earn my pocket-money doing this kind of work on the side. My father pays for my college tuition."

Anna had heard horrible stories from her grandparents about what her country had gone through under Nazi occupation. "So my knowledge of it is more than what I got from books," she said. She was only three months old when the Velvet Revolution brought an end to Communist rule in her country and to its Soviet-satellite status. She made her contempt for communism very obvious when she said, "Unlike my parents, I didn't have the misfortune of growing up under communism."

"Do you know Russian?" I asked her.

"No," she said. "My parents had to learn it. You don't like anything that is forced upon you. Otherwise, I would have gladly learned it. My brother is a medical student. He spent one year in Italy and another one in Portugal as an exchange student. Now he speaks Italian and Portuguese fluently. He plans to learn German and French next. With that, he will have learned four more languages, in addition to Czech, which is our mother tongue, and English that is taught at schools as a second language. I also want to learn as many languages as I can."

I told her to try and get a scholarship to go to one of the Ivy League colleges in the United States. "I am not saying that there is anything wrong with the universities here," I added. "In fact, I don't know anything about Czech universities to make a comparison with American Ivy League institutions. But the fact is a degree from an Ivy League institution opens many doors for you in the job market."

"You are right," she said. "And thank you for those tips. My brother also is of the same opinion. He has been trying to get a scholarship to go to the States. We are not rich. So without some financial help, there is no chance for us to go there."

"Do well in what you are studying now," I told her. "Everything will work out fine for you."

By then, the bus reached Prague, the last stop. We exchanged our email addresses and promised to stay in touch with each other. As we got up, I told Anna, "I was feeling a little depressed when I got on the bus. Some of the exhibits at the Terezin Memorial were too gruesome to watch. You helped me get over the depression. Thank you for the pleasant conversation."

"I enjoyed talking with you too," Anna said. "I feel great. Maybe we are going to meet in the States."

We hugged each other and went our separate ways.

25

A Sikh Victim of Khalistan Movement Happily Settled in Vienna

August 6, 2009 – Thursday

I was on my way from Prague to Vienna by train. There were four other passengers in the six-seat reserved compartment: two girls from a small town in the Czech Republic and a couple from Turin, Italy. The girls had just finished high school and the couple their bachelor's degree.

The girls were planning to go to college, but didn't know what area of studies to specialize in. Also, they hadn't decided what they wanted to be in life. One of them was toying with the idea of becoming a medical doctor. Her grandfather encouraged her to do some traveling before making the final decision.

"You should be proud that you have such a grandfather," I told her. "Not many people in the world are fortunate to receive that kind of advice in their formative years."

Her grandfather even took the trouble of driving both girls from their home town to Prague. He also paid the train fare for the first leg of his granddaughter's journey, from Prague to Vienna. Both girls were very inquisitive about almost everything in the world. I helped them out, to the extent I could, on whatever they wanted to know about India.

By the time we reached Vienna, after four and a half hours,

my fellow passengers, all four of them, had fallen asleep. "That shows how interesting my lecture was," I told them when they woke up. They laughed. We thanked one another for the good time we had on the train and went our separate ways.

This was my second trip to Vienna. The trip last year was by air. At that time, my friend Kulamarva Balakrishna* had come to the airport, accompanied by his son Bharat, to receive me. This time I had told him, before I started from New York, not to bother. I would find my way, on my own, from the train station in Vienna to the bed-and-breakfast place he had booked for me, I had insisted. I was aware of the strict medical regimen Bala, as we close friends called him, had been following since he underwent a major operation to remove his pancreas. He had to take insulin injection every five hours, just to stay alive. I knew first-hand what would happen if he missed one. During my 2008 visit, he nearly collapsed in front of me because, in his enthusiasm to keep me entertained, he had forgotten to take the injection at the scheduled time.

As soon as I got off the train, I headed toward the information window at the station to get direction to the bed-and-breakfast place – or the pension, as they call it in Europe. I had gone only a short distance when a "Namaste" greeting made me stop and turn around. It was from a Sikh news vendor on the platform. He was smiling at me from ear to ear.

"Do you live here or are you just visiting?" he asked me, in Hindi.

When he found me struggling to answer in Hindi, he said that I could speak in English.

To get a little ahead of the story, Kulamarva Balakrishna, an Indian journalist and social activist, passed away on February 27, 2013, in Vienna, Austria, at the age of 78. Vienna had been his home since he left India in 1975, in the wake of the Emergency rule imposed on the country by the late Prime Minister Indira Gandhi. He was one of the few fiercely independent journalists who were shadowed by Mrs. Gandhi's secret police. He left the country when his arrest became imminent. Balakrishna is survived by his Austrian wife Eva and their son Bharat.

"Okay," I told him. "I will speak in English. But you should continue in Hindi. I understand it well. To answer your question, I don't live here. I am a tourist. I will be in Vienna only for three days." I showed him the address of the pension and added, "This is where I will be staying. You could tell me how to get there."

"Oh, it's not far," he said. "You will be there in half an hour."

He told me which train to take, where to get off and which connecting bus to take from there. I thanked him for his help.

"Which part of India are you from?" I asked.

"I am from Punjab," he said.

"Come on," I said, teasingly. Pointing to his turban, I added, "I can tell you are from Punjab. Which part of Punjab?"

He was from Amritsar. He left home over 20 years earlier "when there were troubles back home."

Violent Outbreaks of the 1980s

I immediately knew what he was referring to. He was referring to the violent outbreaks in various parts of Punjab, in the 1980s, caused by Sikh militants fighting for a separate homeland for the Sikhs. The Sikhs constitute two percent of India's population of 1.2 billion. An overwhelming majority of them live in Punjab. The idea for a separate homeland for them was first raised by Sikh exiles living in Britain, Canada and the United States. The movement to create "Khalistan" (the land of the pure), as the separatists called it, turned violent in the 1980s. The violence claimed hundreds of lives.

When Jarnail Singh Bindranwale, the leader of the militant group responsible for the violence, and his fellow militants used the Golden Temple in Amritsar, the Sikh religion's holiest shrine, as a hideout and directed their operations from inside, Indira Gandhi, the then-prime minister of India, ordered the Indian army to flush them out. In the military operation launched by the army, on June 6, 1984, all the militants, including Bindranwale, were killed. Many other Sikhs, who had nothing to do with the militancy but happened to be inside the temple at the time, also lost their lives. According to the Indian government, the death toll in the operation, which it called Operation Blue Star, was 492 Sikhs and 100 army personnel. The Sikhs disputed the figure. According to them, those who died were in the thousands.

The attack on the Golden Temple incensed Sikhs around the world. It was in retaliation for this attack that Prime Minister Gandhi was assassinated, on October 31, 1984, by two Sikh members of her own bodyguard. The assassination led to revenge killings by Mrs. Gandhi's followers in the Congress Party. Thousands of Sikhs across India, but mostly those living in Delhi, lost their lives in the carnage. The Khalistan movement fizzled out when its surviving leaders went underground and eventually left India. Some of them sought refuge in different parts of Europe, including Vienna.

All this went through my mind when the Sikh news vendor living in Vienna said that it was "the troubles back home" that made him leave India. I didn't want to embarrass him by asking whether he was one of those militants who caused the troubles. I refrained from asking it for one more reason: he was too pleasant to be a militant.

I changed the course of our conversation, saying, "Things are quiet back home now. Punjab, once again, is the prosperous state in India which it was before the troubles. Any plan to go back?"

"Not right now," he said. "My two sons are going to school here. They get free education. My wife has a small job in the city government. We have a peaceful life here."

"Do you speak German?" I asked.

"Not well," he said. "But I can manage. The government here sent me to school to learn it. That was also free."

"That's the beauty of this country," I told him. "The government takes good care of its people. Free education, free medical care."

"That's why I am in no hurry to go back. I may think about it once my children are well settled."

Looking at my watch, I said, "I wish I could talk with you for long. My friend is waiting for me. He lives two blocks away from where I will be staying. I promised to have lunch with him."

"Okay," he said, "but please come again before you leave Vienna. Let me get you something to drink. What will you have, tea or coffee?"

"You see, it's very hot outside." Showing the bottle of water I was carrying, I added, "I do have what I need. Maybe next time. We'll meet again."

He smiled and shook hands with me.

"No, he was not one of those Sikh militants who caused troubles in India in the 1980s," I said to myself while walking toward the platform to catch the train. It's quite possible that he was one of the many innocent Sikhs who fled Punjab at the height of the turmoil.

Lunch with Balakrishna

The pension Bala booked for me this time was more elegant and comfortable than the one he had done the previous year. In fact, it was not built to be a pension. It was a family home, part of which was converted into a pension. An Austrian lady, who was in her sixties, owned the place. Her daughter, thirty-something, helped her in running it. Both of them spoke good English. And both of them liked Bala. Part of the reason why they liked him could be that he got them customers now and then. Every time he had visitors from India, he would put them up at this place.

"Bala called a few minutes ago to check whether you had arrived," the owner said, as she opened the door for me.

"He may be hungry," I told her. "I am supposed to have lunch with him. It's already two o'clock."

After a quick shower, I rushed to Bala's apartment. As soon as he opened the door and greeted me with a hug, he said, "Let's have lunch. We'll talk over lunch. Eva [Bala's Austrian wife] was kind enough to prepare it before she left for work. She could not take the day off because there is some special event at her gallery this evening. Both of us are invited. We'll leave around five o'clock." Eva is a painter by profession and works part-time at a city-subsidized art gallery in Vienna.

When I saw the dining room cluttered with Eva's paintings, I told Bala, "Eva knows what is where. Let's not disturb the order or the cheery disorder. Let's eat in the kitchen."

Bala agreed. In the kitchen, over lunch, we talked about everything and everyone of interest to us. In our journalistic days in Bombay, in the late 1960s and early 1970s, we had lots of mutual friends and mutual interests. Bala also told me about the stories he was working on at the moment. He was a tireless blogger. Every day he posted one or two stories on his blog. "What is the point in having knowledge if you don't want to share it with others?" was a refrain he was never tired of repeating.

By six in the evening, we were at Eva's gallery. The gallery hours end at six. On days when there are special events and the premises are used by artists from other disciplines to showcase their talents, both employees of the gallery and visitors to it hang around to watch. On this day, a few young musicians from Vienna, who put together a band, are making a presentation.

"We do it now and then to encourage young talents," Eva told us at the end of the show, over a pizza-and-coke dinner bought by her boss, the manager of the gallery. "If they make any money from the shows," she added, "they contribute part of it to the gallery. The gallery has somehow managed to survive until now on charitable contributions from the public and the subsidy from government."

26

Visit to Austria's Melk Abbey; River Cruise Down the Danube

August 7, 2009 – Friday

My friend Bala had planned to make my visit to Vienna this time more eventful and interesting than the one the previous year. Among the events he planned were a trip to the famous Melk Abbey and a cruise down the Danube River.

The Melk Abbey, named after the town in which it is located, is a massive Benedictine monastery. Melk is a small town – population 5,000, give or take a few dozen – about 37 miles to the west of Vienna. It is in the wine-producing region of Austria, at the western end of the Wachau Valley. It was the original seat of the Babenbergs who ruled Austria before the rise of the House of Habsburgs. The town attained fame as the site of the Melk Abbey. And the Melk Abbey was the reason why Bala decided to take me there.

The cruise he planned would take us from Melk to another small town called Durnstein. After visiting Durnstein, according to the plan, we would be going to nearby Krems and, from there, return to Vienna by train. A few weeks before I left New York, Bala had phoned me up from Vienna and discussed the itinerary. "Whatever you plan is fine with me," I had told him.

The early-morning train ride from Vienna to Melk was very

pleasant. But the pleasantness turned into disappointment when a taxi driver took us for a ride, figuratively speaking. We had made the mistake of asking him, as soon as we came out of the train station, where the famous Melk Abbey was. Instead of telling us that it was just five minutes' walk from where we were standing, he insisted that we take his taxi. He refused to give us direction. After a two-minute ride, we were in front of the abbey. He charged us seven euros. This may sound trivial, but not when you realize that you allowed yourself to be duped by someone.

Largest Ecclesiastical Library

Founded in 1089 in a medieval fortress belonging to the House of Babenberg, the Melk Abbey is still functioning as an abbey and a monastic school. (The school was founded in the 12th century.) We took a quick tour of the interior of the abbey church. The interior, with its stained-glass windows, multi-colored marble, intricate gilding and elaborate frescoes in the dome by Johann Michael Rottmayr, is awe-inspiring.

There is a library attached to the monastery, which became renowned for its extensive manuscript collection. With over 100,000 priceless volumes, including 2,000 manuscripts and 1,600 incunabula, it is said to be the largest ecclesiastical library in the world. In the 15th century, the abbey became the center of the Melk Reform Movement, which reinvigorated the monastic life of Austria and Southern Germany.

The Melk Abbey that the Benedictine monks built in the 11th century was destroyed in a fire in 1297. It was rebuilt many times, and had to withstand a Turkish invasion in the 16th century. Its rebuilding in the present Baroque style was done between 1702 and 1736. Napoleon used the abbey as his headquarters during his Austrian campaign. It survived, almost intact, under the Nazis, following Austria's *anschluss* (union) with Germany (1938), and World War II. But another fire, this one in 1947, damaged it again; and it again required extensive repair. Today, with its 200-foot-high dome and symmetrical, golden-hued bell towers overlooking the Wachau Valley and the Danube River, the abbey is an imposing structure and a great tourist draw. I enjoyed every bit of the tour and thanked Bala for the wonderful time. This joy, however, turned out to be short-lived.

After an alfresco lunch at one of the cafes in the beautiful Abbey Park, we headed to the Danube to begin our cruise. A few minutes' walk from the Melk Abbey was supposed to take us to the passenger pick-up point. But because of the language problem – I know no German and Bala's knowledge of the language was so-so – and because of the wrong information given, unintentionally, by those whom we approached for direction, we ended up walking five kilometers in the hot sun. Needless to say, we missed the boat. We had to take a taxi to catch up with it at the next pick-up point. The taxi cost us 45 euros. I could feel the pinch because it was a waste caused by carelessness.

Wachau Valley's Terraced Vineyards

After a few minutes' cruise down the Danube, enjoying the scenic beauty of the Wachau Valley and its terraced vineyards, we reached Durnstein. The city's name literally means "dry castle" in German. It is said that the name came from the stone castle, which we could see high above the main town area. It was in this castle that King Richard I of England, better known as Richard the Lionheart, was held captive by Duke Leopold V of Austria, after their dispute during the Third Crusade. Until this notorious incident of 1192, Durnstein had been a city that remained in obscurity.

Now, it is a "paradise for those who enjoy getting out on foot," as one travel brochure puts it. All major attractions are within walking distance. The only exception is the old castle, which Bala and I didn't have the time and energy to climb up to. But we did manage to find time to make a quick tour of a gallery that Bala's friends back in Vienna had recommended.

Founded in 1990 by Janusz Pol-Stralkowski and Danuta, both artists themselves, the gallery presented a wide spectrum of their own works. Danuta specialized in realism and impressionism and "Janus," as his friends called him, in abstract and experimental creations. We were disappointed that we didn't have sufficient time to appreciate their works thoroughly.

The last stopover we had planned for the day was Krems, at the confluence of the Danube and the Krems rivers. Because of the earlier blunder, we were left with no time to walk the short distance from Durnstein to Krems and enjoy the beauty of the surrounding areas. We had to take another taxi ride.

Krems's landmarks include the old Stadtburg fortress; the St. Veit parish church, one of Austria's oldest Baroque churches; and two Gothic churches in nearby Stein. Krems, which absorbed Stein in 1938, is also known as a wine-producing town. Austrian and foreign wine connoisseurs congregate in the city, particularly at harvest time in the fall. Bala and I wandered around and took in the beauty of the place as much as we could. A travel brochure we had picked up at the train station describes the place as "a true gem." None would dispute it.

It was 6 p.m. We were waiting at the Krems train station to catch the 6:30 train to Vienna. It struck us as odd that at the train station of a town which has a population of 24,000, we two were the only passengers. To our delightful surprise, it turned out to be to our advantage: The young Somali woman who worked at the station's ticket window engaged us in a pleasant conversation during our half-hour waiting period. The conversation supplemented the bookish knowledge we had about the town.

We were interested in hearing from her more about her personal life than about Krems. "What made you leave Somalia?" I asked her.

"Tribal warfare," she said, "made worse by foreign mercenaries."

At that point, to our disappointment, the train rolled in.

My Thirty-Day European Odyssey

Before we wished her "all the best" and rushed to the platform, she managed to squeeze in one more sentence: "I am very happy to be in Austria."

That made our journey back to Vienna happy too. On balance, the day was not a total disaster.

27

Flight to Frankfurt; Parting Gift from a German Fellow Passenger

August 8, 2009 – Saturday

I was at Vienna's main bus station. My plan was to take an early-morning bus to Bratislava, the capital of Slovakia, and fly by Ryanair from Bratislava to Frankfurt. Bala and Eva came to the bus station to see me off, in spite of my repeated requests not to.

When the bus arrived, Eva handed me a paper bag containing something and said, "I have not been a good hostess to you this time. I did not have time to cook for you and treat you to a decent lunch or dinner. Here is some breakfast that I prepared for you. Please have it on your way."

I was touched. During the two-hour bus ride, I remembered the pleasant time I had in Vienna in the previous three days. That Eva had not been a good hostess to me this time was the last thing I had on my mind. In fact, she had done more than what one could expect from her, given her tight schedule. She had been busy organizing special shows at the art gallery where she worked and preparing for an exhibition of her own paintings. Bala and I would drop by the gallery whenever our wandering around the city took us to its neighborhood. And whenever we did, Eva more than made up for not being a good hostess at home: she would take a break from work and join us in our wandering for at least for a couple of hours. All this made Eva's apology unnecessary.

Sitting next to me on the bus was Monika. She would be taking the same Ryanair flight to Frankfurt as me. She was from a small town – I had not heard the town's name before – close to Germany's border with Luxembourg. A primary school teacher by profession, she spoke good English. One of the subjects she taught was English, she told me.

"When I decided to study English thirty-five years ago, I was a rarity in my town," she said. "We Germans have belatedly recognized the need to learn foreign languages, especially English."

"The same is the case with Americans," I told her. "It took a war for them to give up their stupid belief that there was no need to learn any language other than English – American English, I mean – as long as their country remained the only superpower in the world."

When the bus arrived at the Bratislava airport, Monika and I went straight to the Ryanair counter. We found, after we completed our check-in formalities, that we had more than an hour to kill before boarding. We picked a quiet corner in the waiting area and started unwinding.

I opened the bag of breakfast Eva had given me. It contained toasted bread, fried eggs and bacon, two apples and one liter of pineapple juice. "This is more than sufficient for two people," I told Monika. "Why don't you join me?"

"No, thank you," she said. "I had a heavy breakfast."

"But this is not just any breakfast," I told her. "It comes with a lot of love."

I narrated the story behind it.

"You have some wonderful friends," Monika said. "And I envy you. But there is only so much that my stomach can take. Let me make you feel good. I will take an apple."

I ate as much as I could. "I hate wasting food, especially this, to which I am sentimentally attached," I said to Monika, as I was throwing the leftover in the nearby dumpster.

I held on to the bottle of juice and started sipping it now and then. When I noticed Monika reaching for the bottle of water she had in her bag, I said, "Why drink water when you have pineapple juice? Didn't Mary Antoinette tell her people something like that?"

"Your analogy is a little far-fetched," she said, laughing. "I am sure you agree with me that for a thirsty person, sweet juice is no substitute for water, no matter how sentimentally attached you are to it."

Our pleasant exchange was interrupted by an announcement from Ryanair, asking us to proceed for security clearance. I looked at the bottle I was holding. It was still more than half-full. Post-9/11 restrictions prohibit passengers from carrying any liquid on board. Feeling guilty about throwing it away, I asked some of the passengers standing near me whether they were thirsty.

"This is something special," I told them and repeated the story, which Monika was tired of hearing by then. I also told them: "But for the post-Osama bin Laden restrictions, I would be holding on to this bottle until I drank the last drop in it."

They all laughed. "You are being mushy," one of them said. But none would take even a drop of the juice. I felt really bad when I put it in a nearby receptacle.

"If Osama bin Laden could witness this, he would be deriving great sadistic pleasure," I said, as I emptied my pants' pocket, removed the belt and shoes and put them in a tray.

How Low-Cost Airlines Keep Cost Low

Monika and I had managed to get adjoining seats while checking in. Once the plane took off, she started asking lots of questions about India. "India is my next travel destination," she told me. "That's why I am asking all these questions."

"I thought so," I told her.

After we got off the plane, she accompanied me to the bus-stop to make sure that I boarded the right bus to the city. She didn't have to take any bus or taxi. She had driven her own car to the airport four days earlier and left it in the paid-parking area. "I am going in the opposite direction," she told me. "Otherwise, I would have given you a ride."

This was the first time I flew by Ryanair. I learned how low-cost airlines were able to keep their fares so low. One of the ways in which they do it is by operating from airports that are far away from the city. The fee paid for operations at such airports is much lower than what busy airports, especially busy international airports, charge.

However, for passengers, the deal is not all that attractive. They end up spending for travels between far-away airports and the cities almost as much as they save on airfare. And a lot of time is wasted on those airport-to-city travels.

The Frankfurt-Hahn Airport, which super-cheap airlines like Ryanair use, is not in Frankfurt. It is in the Mosel region, 70 miles away from Frankfurt. Airlines add "Frankfurt" to the airport's name to make their offer attractive to passengers going to Frankfurt.

While taking leave of me, Monika, in addition to a kiss on the cheek, gave me a small gift. The gift was a bead she said she had picked up in Istanbul. "This is Fatima's eye," she said, pointing to the picture on the bead. And added, "Do you know who Fatima is?"

"Born and brought up in a country which has the third-largest Muslim population in the world," I told her, "I should know who Fatima is."

"The Prophet Muhammad's daughter is going to bring you lots of luck," she said and walked toward her car in the parking lot.

After two hours' ride, the bus reached its final stop, outside Frankfurt's main train station. As soon as I got off the bus, I went inside the station, which travel books say is the busiest train station in Germany.

Built in the 1890s, the station now serves, on average, about 350,000 travelers a day. On weekdays, it handles 1,800 trains, arriving at and departing from its 24 platforms. The station was teeming with people, mostly tourists, when I arrived there in the afternoon. The energy in the atmosphere made me forget the boredom I had felt during the two-hour bus journey. Another factor that made me feel good was that the hostel I had booked was only a couple of minutes' walk from the train station.

The day was so bright that I didn't want to spend the rest of it inside my tiny room at the hostel. After a quick shower, I got out and started exploring Frankfurt right away. I had prepared a tentative list of all the important places I wanted to visit during the three days I would be staying in the city.

Why Frankfurt Is Nicknamed Mainhattan

Frankfurt's official, German name is Frankfurt am Main, meaning Frankfurt on the Main. The Main River, which is a tributary of the Rhine River, runs through Frankfurt toward the end of its 326-mile course. It divides the city into northern and southern parts. The southern part is mostly forest, the largest forest within any city in Germany. That makes Frankfurt the greenest city in Germany. The hub of the city is on the north side of the Main. All the skyscrapers built in the post-World War II period, giving Frankfurt a Manhattan-like skyline, are located here. As one can tell, Frankfurt's nickname, Mainhattan, is a portmanteau derived from the Main and Manhattan.

Until World War II, Frankfurt's Old Town had been the largest medieval city in Germany that still remained intact. The Allied bombing campaign, in 1944, destroyed most of it. It was rebuilt later. Though the rebuilt Frankfurt has many modern high-rise buildings, all the historical structures have been carefully restored to their original forms. Among the most famous historical landmarks are the Romer ("the Roman," formerly the site of the Holy Roman Emperor's coronation, and now the seat of the Frankfurt City Hall); St. Bartholomew's Cathedral, also known as the red stone cathedral; and St. Paul's Church (*Paulskirche*), which was the meeting place of the first Frankfurt National Assembly.

My Thirty-Day European Odyssey

As I came out of the hostel, I could see that the neighborhood, especially the area around the main train station, was lively. I could also see that it was reflective of the multiethnic, multicultural composition of Frankfurt. About 30 percent of the city's 700,000 residents are foreign-born. They say Frankfurt's economic growth is fueled by the entrepreneurial spirits of its immigrant population. The proof of it was very much there in the immediate vicinity of the hostel.

There were three tiny restaurants on the same street as the hostel. All of them were owned by Arabs and sold Middle-Eastern foods – kebab, falafel, hummus, etc. One was owned by a handsome Egyptian couple, 30-something. Both husband and wife worked there 14 to 16 hours a day, seven days a week. "We are not complaining," the wife hastened to add. "The country has been good to us."

Two storefronts away from the Egyptian restaurant was another one, owned by a middle-aged Iraqi. His wife and daughter helped him whenever they could, he said. Neither of them was there at the time I walked in. They had to juggle, he said, between work at home and work at the restaurant. The wife had more work at home because she had to take care of their three school-going sons, ages seven, nine and 12. The daughter, the eldest of their four children, got married recently. "More time with husband means less time at the restaurant," he said, with a smile. "It's not easy being an immigrant," he added.

The Iraqi restaurateur struck me as an interesting person. I wanted to talk with him more. "We'll meet again," I said, while shaking hands with him. "May be tomorrow."

Another eatery, a few feet away, had a huge board placed in front of it. The board was too big for the place, which was just a hole in the wall. The board had "Mediterranean Cuisine" written on it, in large letters. The place was owned by a Lebanese, who had left his home town, Beirut, nearly three decades earlier, "when Israeli bombings destroyed everything I had – my home, my restaurant, everything."

He was referring to Israel's 1982 invasion of Lebanon, which had invited world-wide condemnation, including from its closest ally, the United States. "I clearly remember those bombings," I told him. "We'll talk about it some other time. I am here two more days."

I might have walked for a minute or so when a convenience store owned by a Nepali caught my attention. He welcomed me in with a broad smile and warm handshake. He said he had been in Frankfurt for seven years. He was married and had a one-year-old son. He could be in his late twenties or early thirties. "Until two years ago, the business was good," he said. "Now it is …" Instead of completing the sentence, he pointed his thumb downward.

"What you are going through is what businesses all over the world have been experiencing lately," I told him. "But things are beginning to change for the better. It won't be too long before you feel the change yourself. Hang in there. I am sure you will make it in this country."

On the next block, closer to the train station, was an Internet café, owned by an Indian-looking man. When he said he was from Sri Lanka, I could immediately conclude that he was one of those Sri Lankan Tamils who fled the country when the civil war broke out. I wanted to talk about it. But the place was crowded and he was busy taking care of customers. I spent about half an hour there, checking my emails and browsing some of my favorite news sites. While leaving, I thanked the Sri Lankan and said, "See you tomorrow."

I knew I was going to see him the next day. I had a lot to talk about. I wanted to hear from him about the 25-year-long civil war in his country that was still going on. I had a long day and was getting tired. So I decided to get back to the hostel.

There were two girls sitting in the foyer of the hostel, playing some computer game on their laptops and talking in Portuguese. I asked them where they were from. When they said they were from Rio de Janeiro, I told them about the wonderful time I had in their hometown, in 2001. I talked with them until I could no longer keep my eyes open. Then, reluctantly, I said "good night" and retired to my room.

28

Tamil Victim of Sri Lanka's Civil War Struggling to Make It in Frankfurt

August 9, 2009 – Sunday

It was my first full day in Frankfurt. Determined to utilize every minute of it, I left the hostel at about 8 a.m. I was armed with a map of Frankfurt and a few travel brochures.

I also had with me a 5.80-euro city tour pass, which would allow me to take bus, tram or subway train in the city's public transportation system any number of times. It would be valid for 24 hours from its first use. I also planned to walk as much as my energy level would permit, enjoying the sights and sounds of the city.

As I passed by the Sri Lankan-owned Internet café, I saw the man, with whom I had a brief conversation the day before, coming out the door with a bucket and a mop in hand. He was going to clean the windows, he said.

"Nobody to help you?" I asked him.

"My wife comes here around noon. She takes care of customers. This kind of manual work I do myself. Maybe sometime in the future we'll be able to hire some help. Not right now."

What he said reminded me of what I heard from a few Sri Lankans I had met in Paris, Oslo and Stockholm – husband-and-wife teams struggling to set up small businesses. I told him about it, adding, "They too are victims of what is going on back in your country. There is no end in sight."

I was referring to the latest turn of events in the 25-year-long civil war between the Tamil Tigers and the Sri Lankan Army. The latest news said that the fighting had intensified; that casualties had been mounting; and that more and more Tamils had been fleeing the war zone. It also said that the Sri Lankan president, Mahinda Rajapaksa, rejected another cease-fire request, this one from Prime Ministers Gordon Brown of Britain. It seemed Rajapaksa, emboldened by the steady gains his troops had been making, was determined to fight to the end. He had become sure of winning the war. That many innocent civilians were getting killed in the process didn't seem to bother him. All this went through my mind when I stood in front of the Sri Lankan Tamil who was struggling to make it in Frankfurt.

"It is too depressing to hear about what is going on there," he said. That made me change the topic. I told him that I was going to wander around the city all day.

"Start wandering from that point," he said, pointing to Kaiserstrasse, the beautiful for-pedestrians-only boulevard, beyond the traffic island in front of the train station.

"I will come back in the evening to check my email," I told him. "We'll talk more. Be optimistic. You have a future in this country."

He thanked me for those "kind words."

As I was walking toward Kaiserstrasse, I saw five Oriental-looking girls taking pictures, with the train station in the background. Each was taking pictures of the other four on all five cameras. It was fun to watch them making different hand gestures for each picture.

When they finished 25 snaps, I approached them and said, "Don't you want a picture of all of you together?"

"Yes," all of them said in unison, excited at my offer. They handed me their cameras.

I got their pictures on all five cameras. To my bemusement,

this time also they made different hand gestures for different pictures. I didn't ask them what those gestures meant.

"Check whether the pictures came out OK," I told them, handing back their cameras. "Otherwise, I can go another round."

Each of them gave me a thumbs-up.

"Are you from Thailand?" I asked them.

"No, Taiwan," all of them said, again in unison, and in a tone that made clear that they didn't like my identifying them as Thais.

"I am sorry," I said. "You look Thai to me. Didn't mean to offend you. By the way, what is so offensive about being Thai?"

"No, sir," one of the girls said. "We are not offended. We are only showing our pride in being Taiwanese."

All of them were college students from Taipei, the capital of Taiwan, enjoying a two-week summer vacation around Europe. Frankfurt was their first stop.

When they said that they were proud of being Taiwanese, I almost asked whether they were proud of being Chinese too. That would have been my way of finding out whether they supported the small minority in Taiwan that advocates its merger with mainland China or the majority that wants to maintain its independent status. On second thoughts, I decided not to ask, fearing that I would unnecessarily be crossing over to a politically sensitive area. One day, the issue would have to be resolved between the two groups, I said to myself.

"Enjoy your vacation," I told them, shook hands with each and waved good-bye. I continued my walk toward Kaiserstrasse.

Chat with a Pakistani Restaurateur

Kaiserstrasse, with many old buildings built in the 1890s, has an old-world charm. It also has some inexpensive restaurants. One of them is Pakistani-owned. I couldn't resist going in and taking a look.

"I just had my breakfast," I told the man sitting at the cash register. "When I saw the board, I couldn't help coming in to say hello."

When he told me that he was also the owner of the place, I gave him a congratulatory handshake. He and most of the workers there were from Karachi. We talked for a few minutes. He kept insisting that I have something. "I have Darjeeling tea," he said.

"Maybe later," I told him. "I will come back. Right now, let me go around and enjoy Frankfurt. This is my first full day in the city."

He told me to avoid a couple of streets in the neighborhood. "Unless you are hungry for that," he added. "You know what I am talking about."

I knew exactly what he was talking about. He was talking about the brothels and strip clubs in the area. Most of them came up soon after World War II, when 30,000 U.S. troops were stationed in Frankfurt. Frankfurters don't complain about the brothels and strip clubs so much. Their complaint is about the Russian mob that moved in when the U.S. troops left.

Frankfurt is one of the oldest trade-fair cities in the world. The practice of hosting trade fairs started in 1240, when the authorities promised safe passage to all participating merchants. Now, the city hosts about 51 trade fairs and exhibitions every year. *Messe*, the convention center that hosts them, is so vast that it can accommodate 40 soccer fields.

Side by side with trade shows, the city's prostitution industry also flourished. (Prostitution is legal in Frankfurt, as in many other German cities.) The trend in the prostitution industry closely follows the theme of the trade show. Prostitutes have a boom time during auto shows, while they nearly starve during book fairs. Frankfurt's annual book fair is world-famous. Book lovers and bookstore owners from all over the world flock to the city during the fair season. But they flock with a different kind of hunger, which prostitutes cannot satisfy.

When I told the Karachi restaurateur about the nature of trade fair determining the trend in the city's flesh trade, he laughed.

"Isn't it true in our countries also?" he asked. "Of course, we don't have book fairs comparable to that of Frankfurt. But we have festivals throughout the year. That's the time prostitutes do flourishing business in our countries."

"We can keep on talking like this till cows come home," I told him. "But I have many other interesting places to visit. You made my day."

Banking District

My next destination was the Banking District, the area in which the banking culture of Frankfurt is vibrant now. Long before Frankfurt became the banking capital of Europe, it had earned the nickname Bankfurt.

The city's banking culture began with the Rothschild banking dynasty, which in turn began with its founder, Mayer Amschel Rothschild. Born on February 23, 1744, in the Jewish ghetto of Frankfurt, he became the richest banker in the world before he died on September 19, 1812.

The area now known as the Banking District is also associated with many other historic events. By the time World War II ended, Germany's economy was in a shambles. The reichsmark, the currency of the country under the Nazis, had ceased to be of any value. It was replaced with the deutsche mark. Under the U.S.-sponsored Marshall Plan, the U.S. printed large quantities of the new currency and injected them into the German economy. The Marshall Plan, which played a key role in rebuilding the German economy, was implemented from the Banking District.

My next stop was at the Main Tower, which headquarters the Helaba Bank. From the public-view platform on the top of the tower, one gets a panoramic view of all of Frankfurt. To reach the platform, situated 650 feet above ground, one has to take an elevator up to the building's 54th floor and then walk up 50 stairs.

A couple of blocks away from the Main Tower is the famous *Alte Oper* (the opera house) of Frankfurt. The original *Alte*

Oper, which the German king, Kaiser Wilhelm I, inaugurated on October 20, 1880, was destroyed in the Allied bombings during World War II. On March 23, 1944, to be exact. The rubble to which it was reduced was preserved as "Germany's most beautiful ruin," when debate went on over whether to rebuild it or not.

At last, largely on the initiative of Frankfurt residents, and "over the objections of a mayor nicknamed Dynamite Rudi," a decision was made in favor of rebuilding it. The new opera house, which Frankfurters say is true to its original form, was inaugurated on August 28, 1981.

Since then, the *Alte Oper* has been the venue for nearly 300 concerts and other events every year. The other events include conferences, receptions and anniversary galas organized by private companies and institutions.

It was past 2 p.m., and I was feeling hungry. I couldn't think of a better place to have a quick bite than the nearby "Pig-Out Alley." This street also is set aside only for pedestrians. The actual name of the street is Grosse Bockenheimer Strasse, but Frankfurters call it *Fressgass*. Travel writers like Rick Steves have translated the word into English as the "Feeding Street," which Frankfurters find too bland. Their preferred translation is the "Pig-Out Alley." After watching tourists and locals wolfing down foods they bought at cheap Chinese, Greek, Middle Eastern and other eateries, and at fast-food places like McDonald's, I found myself in agreement with the translation preferred by Frankfurters: the "Pig-Out Alley."

Maybe, there is another reason for their preference. It may have something to do with the sausage Frankfurt is famous for. They say the highest-quality sausage in the world is made in Frankfurt. The original name of what Americans call hot dog is frankfurter. I am not a big fan of frankfurter. "But when in Frankfurt, eat frankfurter," I said to myself and ordered a couple of them at a nearby wheelbarrow outlet. The Frankfurt-made frankfurter did taste better.

St. Paul's Church

The next place on my wish list for the day was St. Paul's Church. The German name for St. Paul's Church is *Paulskirche*. Though it was started as a place of worship by Lutherans, in 1789, it soon became a place very much associated with German politics. By 1848, it had become the seat of the first democratically elected German National Assembly. The first German Constitution, which paved the way for a united Germany in 1871, was drafted in the hall of St. Paul's Church. That's why the church is also called the "cradle of German democracy."

In 1913, during the centennial of the Napoleonic Wars, the church was officially designated as a memorial site. Like many other historical buildings in Frankfurt, the original St. Paul's Church was destroyed in the 1944 Allied bombings.

Its reconstruction began soon after the war. The newly built structure was consecrated on May 18, 1948, on the occasion of the centennial celebrations of the German National Assembly. Today, it is used as a venue for various exhibitions and other events. The most popular annual event is the awarding of the Peace Prize of the German Book Trade, which takes place during the famous Frankfurt Book Fair.

St. Paul's Church was one of the places U.S. President John F. Kennedy chose to visit during his famous 1963 tour of West Germany. On June 25, 1963, he gave a rousing speech to the packed-to-overflowing crowd in the church's 900-seat assembly hall.

As I came out of the church, I reminded myself that it was not the speech delivered here that President Kennedy's 1963 visit to West Germany was famous for. It was the one he delivered the next day, in West Berlin, in the Rudolph Wilde Platz near the Berlin Wall, which ended with these memorable words: *"Ich bin ein Berliner* [I am a Berliner]."

I left the premises repeating those words.

29

What Frankfurt Was Like in Medieval Times

August 10, 2009 – Monday

Frankfurt is one of Europe's oldest cities. To get a feel of what the city was like in medieval times, when it was built, one has to go to the Old Town *(Altstadt)* area of the city, the area around the city's market square. The beautiful market square is called Romerberg. Few tourists to Frankfurt end their tour without paying a visit to Romerberg. My turn to do it came on this day.

Romerberg gets its name from its 15th-century *Romer* or the town hall. It was called *Romer* because, before it became the Frankfurt Town Hall, it was the lodging place for Roman merchants visiting the city to participate in its trade fairs. It became the town hall only in 1405.

The town hall also houses the *Kaisersaal*, or the Imperial Hall, in which Holy Roman Emperors conducted their coronation ceremonies. The trade fairs and book fairs, which Frankfurt is famous for, began in Romerberg and moved to their present location later.

Another attractive building in the square is the Gothic red-and-white Old Nikolai Church (*Alte Nikolaikirche*, in German), originally built in 1290. The attractive, half-timbered buildings that we see in the square today were houses once upon a time.

They now house expensive bars and restaurants. The original church and buildings, and most other medieval structures in the city, were destroyed in the 1944 Allied bombings. What we see today are faithful reproductions, completed in 1983, of what existed in the 15th and 16th centuries.

There is another structure in the square that every visitor would find amusing: the Fountain of Justice. First built in sandstone in 1611, it was rebuilt in bronze in 1887. It shows a woman with a sword in her right hand and scales (symbolizing justice) in the other. Below her are statues of a few other women, with water spouting from their mouths and nipples. There are also a few male statues, with water spouting only from their mouths. "The sculptor was careful not to show water spouting through any other porous parts of the male body," a tourist was heard whispering to his friend.

All history buffs would find the metal plaque in the square, which commemorates the notorious Nazi book-burning of May 10, 1933, fascinating. A quote from the famous German poet Heinrich Heine, about the despicable act of book-burning, is engraved around the edge of the plaque. The quote is in German. Its English translation is as follows: "That was mere foreplay. Where they have burned books, they will end in burning human beings."

How prescient Heine was! He wrote those words in 1820. The Nazi book-burning that took place a little over a century later was, indeed, the "foreplay" of the Holocaust that followed.

Germany has come a long way since then. The efforts it has made to put its Nazi past behind it are laudable. Musing about those efforts, I walked toward the next historical place on my itinerary, St. Bartholomew's Cathedral.

Kaiserdom

Frankfurt's St. Bartholomew's Cathedral, strictly speaking, is not a cathedral. It has never been the seat of a Catholic bishop. In 1250, a church was ordered to be constructed at the site of a seventh-century Merovingian chapel. When the church, the fifth one to be built on the same site, was completed, it was dedicated to St. Bartholomew.

In 1356, Charles IV, the king of Germany who also held the title of the Holy Roman Emperor, issued a Golden Bull decreeing that the church be used to elect and crown successive German kings from then onward. Until then, they were selected, not elected, and crowned in Rome by the pope. Charles IV himself was crowned in Rome. Why, only a few months after his own coronation by the pope, he issued a bull challenging papal authority over Germany's political affairs is a mystery to many in the Catholic Church. Be that as it may, since the issuance of the 1356 Golden Bull, all German kings were elected and crowned at St. Bartholomew's Cathedral, in Frankfurt. From 1562, all Holy Roman Emperors were also crowned here. That's how the place came to be called the Kaiserdom or the Emperor's Cathedral.

The original church was destroyed in a devastating fire in 1867. It was rebuilt in 1880, only to be destroyed again, this time in the World War II Allied bombings. It took four years, 1950 through 1953, for German authorities to rebuild the Kaiserdom into the marvelous Gothic structure that we see today.

It has a symmetrical, cross-shaped floor plan. The high altar at the center of the choir is decorated with a fine Gothic retable from the second half of the 15th century. The Maria-Schlaf-Altar, in the Mary Chapel, was created in 1434. It shows a dying Virgin Mary surrounded by the Apostles. It is among the few original pieces that survived World War II bombings.

Then, there is the small vaulted room called Election Chapel. Seven princes from different parts of Germany, who constituted the electoral college, gathered in this small room whenever they had to elect a new emperor. Sixteen out of the 23 German emperors were elected here.

The cathedral's Gothic tower, added in the 15th century, has 312 steps, reaching a height of 312 feet. One gets a good view of the city from the top of the tower. But the view is nothing, compared with what one gets from the top of the Main Tower in the Banking District. So if you are too tired to climb the steps, skip visiting this tower. Another reason why you should do it: You have to pay to enter the tower, though entry to the cathedral itself is free.

Another part of the Kaiserdom where you have to pay to gain entry is the Dom-Museum. Paying for it is not worth it, because the archaeological findings and relics related to the history of the church that are displayed here are not all that impressive. The only exceptions are the objects from a Merovingian grave unearthed from the cathedral's central nave.

Before leaving the Old Town area, I decided to visit a couple of other important places that were on my wish list. One was the Goethe House (*Goethehaus* in German), which was only five minutes' walk from where I was standing.

Goethe House

"As the bells tolled noon" – that's how Johann Wolfgang von Goethe describes his birth, on August 28, 1749, in *Poetry and Truth,* his autobiography. As I entered the Goethe House, I was aware that it was not the actual house in which he was born and had lived until the age of 26. (He moved to Weimar when he was 26 and died there, on March 22, 1832.) That house also was destroyed during the World War II bombings.

However, after visiting the Goethe House, I was convinced that the claims made in the booklet I had in my hand – that "the house has been faithfully restored to the original" and that the "furnishings of the kitchen, living room and reception rooms correspond" to the bourgeois lifestyle of the late baroque period – were legitimate. The visit to the Goethe House was worth every cent of the seven-euro entrance fee I paid.

Goethe was not just a poet; he was also a playwright, a novelist, a scientist, a statesman, a theater director, a critic, and an amateur artist. It is said that his collection of 2,000 books was sold off in 1795. More than half of them have been traced and repurchased in recent decades. To get an idea of what made

Goethe the greatest German literary figure of the modern era, one only has to visit his study, which is on the second floor of the house.

One of the items that survived World War II bombings is an astronomical clock. This unique memento, dating back to 1746, is now displayed on the third floor of the house. On the top floor are Goethe's puppet theater and a private room. We were told that Goethe started working on *Faust* in this room, when he was 23. *Faust,* a tragic play in two parts, was written over a period of 30 years. It is not only Goethe's masterpiece but also one of the greatest works in German literature.

The Goethe Museum is on the ground floor. It has, among other things, a picture gallery dedicated to the Age of Goethe. The pictures, apart from showing Goethe at various ages, bear testimony to his relationship with artists like Johann Heinrich Füssli and Caspar David Friedrich.

Museum Judengasse and Jewish Cemetery

As I came out of the Goethe House, I realized that I didn't have enough time to visit all the remaining places on my wish list. But being a student of history, I couldn't bring myself to leave the neighborhood without visiting some of the places that are inextricably linked to Frankfurt's history. I am talking about the Museum Judengasse, the Jewish Cemetery and the Jewish Museum. The first two were about five minutes' walk from where I was. I headed toward them.

Before World War II, there were 30,000 Jews living in Frankfurt. The most prominent Jewish family was the Rothschilds. Before the war, Jews were allowed to live only in the ghetto. Today, there are about 8,000 Jews, and they are spread all over the city. The Museum Judengasse was built on the excavated remains of what was once the Jewish ghetto. It was opened in 1992.

Judengasse in German means Jews' alley. It was the main street of the ghetto, and was outside the walls of the city. The Frankfurt authorities moved the Jewish community into the ghetto in 1462, and kept them there until around 1810. Inside the Museum Judengasse, there are numerous pictures showing what life was like in that ghetto. One would be surprised to learn that, by the 1700's, over 3,000 Jews lived in that cramped space. The foundations of 19 old houses were discovered at the site during a 1977 archaeological excavation. Five of them are on display in the museum now.

The Jewish Cemetery, which is the second-oldest in Germany, is behind the Museum Judengasse. It is closed to the public. Peeking through its closed gate, one can see on the ground the surviving gravestones dating from 1270. The most famous gravestone is that of Mayer Amschel Rothschild, the founder of the Rothschild dynasty.

The cemetery's main attraction is the Holocaust Memorial Wall, with 12,000 tiny memorials on it. Engraved on the metal pieces that serve as memorials are the names of Frankfurt Jews killed in the Holocaust. One piece is dedicated to Anne Frank. She was born in Frankfurt, in 1929, and her family later moved to Amsterdam.

Another place that commemorates the city's Jewish past is the Jewish Museum. Housed in the former Rothschild family palace, it is a few blocks away from the cemetery. As I was pressed for time, I decided to skip it. There was another reason for skipping it: I was told that all the exhibits in the museum were described only in German, and I couldn't afford to hire an interpreter.

My next destination was the European Central Bank. I got on the train to the next stop, Willy-Brandt-Platz (named for the late West German Chancellor).

The European Central Bank

The European Central Bank (ECB) occupies most of the 840,000-square-foot-area of the 40-story, 486-foot-tall Eurotower. The ECB, established in 1998 by the Treaty of Amsterdam, administers the monetary policy of the European Monetary

Union, also known as the Eurozone. The Eurozone countries are members of the European Union that have adopted euro as their national currency.

Perched on tall concrete pillars, outside the Eurotower, is a huge euro symbol, cast in metal. There are stars around and inside the symbol. The number of stars indicated the number of countries that joined the Eurozone. When I saw that there were only 12 stars, it aroused my curiosity. "As of today, the EU has twenty-seven members," I said to myself. "Sixteen of them have joined the Eurozone. Shouldn't the number of stars be sixteen?"

To get an answer, and also to find out what the ECB looked like from inside, I decided to go in.

There is a bookstore, owned by the bank, on one side of the main entrance. I stopped by the store and browsed through some of the books and brochures published by the bank. There was nobody else in the store at the time, other than its manager, a pleasant-looking young woman. I couldn't pass up the opportunity to chat with her. "I know that when the European Monetary Union was established, only twelve EU members joined it," I told her. "But now the Eurozone has 16 members. Do you think the number of stars on the euro symbol outside will be increased to sixteen soon?"

"I don't think so," she said. "Maybe someone from the bank can give you a more reliable answer. Why don't you go in and try?"

"That's what I am going to do," I told her and went out of the store.

There was a guard at the bank's main entrance. When I told him the purpose of my visit, his response was: "No question from the public is entertained."

"That's very strange, sir," I told him. I explained, as politely as I could, that a prestigious institution like the ECB should have someone to answer legitimate questions from the public. Pointing to the reception desk which I could see through the glass door, I said, "Would you mind if I go to that lady and talk to her. It will take only a minute."

"No question from the public is entertained," he repeated, this time with more firmness. He had a smile on his face when he uttered those words, both times. The smile didn't sit well on the face of a person, who was about seven-foot-tall and with the weight to match. If anything, it made him more intimidating. He towered over me during the couple of minutes I stood before him. I dared not argue with him.

As I left the building, I said to myself, "The stature of the man does match the steadily increasing strength of the euro and the imposing building in which the European Central Bank functions. The bank deserves praise for recruiting the right man for the right job."

I decided to call it a day. My hostel was at walking distance from Willy-Brandt-Platz. While passing by the Pakistani restaurant, I recalled the promise I had given to its owner during my pleasant chat with him the day before: that I would visit the place again. Also, I had to pick up something to eat. I walked in.

I saw the same owner sitting at the cash register. Unlike last time, the place now had several customers, most of them foreigners. The owner greeted me with a warm smile and handshake, and said, "Good to see you again. No excuse this time. You must have something – some German beer, Darjeeling tea?"

I settled for Darjeeling tea. "I also want to pick up something," I said. "I would have eaten it here. But I badly need to take a shower before I eat. Let me order a chicken biryani. I will eat it at the hostel."

"No problem, sir. We'll make it special for you."

A waiter brought the tea. The owner made me sit by his side and started chatting. The waiter – who, like the owner, was from Karachi – wanted to join us in the chat. He hung around, but when a customer raised his hand to call his attention, he shook hands with me and left. I could see he was disappointed.

Sipping Darjeeling tea, I had another round of pleasant conversation with the restaurateur from Karachi. He was a very politically conscious person. He told me about the political turmoil in Pakistan and about the struggles he went through soon after he arrived in Frankfurt. Our conversation ended when another waiter brought me a bag containing the biryani and a few side dishes.

The problem now was to get the owner to accept payment for the meal. "It's my treat, it's my treat," he kept saying every time I put the money on the table.

"You have already treated me," I told him. "The conversation I had with you is the best treat I have had in all of Frankfurt."

Finally, when I threatened to walk out leaving the biryani behind, he took part of the money I had placed on the table. I didn't think he charged me the full price of the meal. He gave me a hug and asked me to "come back to Frankfurt again."

"I will," I said, "especially if you are going to be here."

I walked back to the hostel with a sweet taste in my mouth. The disappointing experience I had with the guard at the European Central Bank had become a distant memory.

30

Flight from Frankfurt to Oslo, with Two Pakistani Sisters by My Side

August 11, 2009 – Tuesday

It was 8 a.m. I had two more hours at my disposal before bidding farewell to Frankfurt. I got out of the hostel, hoping to enjoy the beauty of Frankfurt for one last time.

Most shops were still closed. A man was standing in front of one that was half-shuttered. It was a souvenir shop, and there was no mistaking that he was its owner. I approached him and said, "I am a tourist and I will be leaving the city in two hours. Could I pick up something for the memory of my visit to Frankfurt, something that is truly representative of the city?"

"I open the shop only at nine," the man said. "But because you say it is for memory, I don't mind making an exception."

He pushed the shutter all the way up and let me in. "Take a look," he said.

I took a quick glance of various items displayed on the shelves. When the shop-owner found me confused about what to pick, he decided to help me out. Handing me a replica in bronze of Romerberg, he said, "Do you like it?"

"I cannot think of anything more representative of Frankfurt than Romerberg," I told him. "Thank you for helping me save some time."

The price was right too: just eight euros. I bought it, thanked the shop-owner and continued my wandering.

In a few minutes, I was at Willy-Brandt Platz, again. Again I found myself standing in front of the giant euro symbol perched on concrete pillars. The symbol and the 12 stars embossed on it shone brighter in the morning sun. The mammoth building nearby that houses the European Central Bank brought back to mind the unpleasant encounter I had with the guard. I dared not try to enter the building this time.

I was anxious, though, to have a picture of me taken, with the euro symbol in the background. A passerby helped me capture one on my camera. That was the last picture that recorded my 2009 Frankfurt visit.

I went back to the hostel, picked up my bag and left for Frankfurt-Hahn Airport, to catch another Ryanair flight, this time to Oslo.

Well before the check-in time, a representative of Ryanair came to the waiting area and invited the passengers to weigh their bags so they could "save a lot of time at the check-in counter." She was standing in front of a weighing machine. The no-frills Ryanair allows only one bag, not exceeding 15 kilograms in weight, to be checked in free of charge. A few kilograms in excess could cost the passengers more than the price of the ticket.

Most passengers – myself included – were aware of this baggage regulation and careful to pack the bags accordingly. The airlines representative cleared our bags in no time, repeating a joke now and then: "Go and do some more shopping."

The bags of some passengers exceeded the limit, but only by a kilogram or two. It was easy for them to take out a few items and put them in their cabin bag.

Turkish Woman's Excess Baggage

In the case of a Turkish woman, it was not that easy. She had to empty almost half the bag. During the emptying process, she took her bag back to the Ryanair representative at least three times, only to be told each time that she had to take out some more items.

Her cabin bag was already filled to capacity. So she had to find other ways of carrying the items that came out of the bag that was to be checked in. It was fun to watch how she did it. She was a heavyset woman and already had an ankle-length tunic on. She put three more tunics on top of it. Then she wrapped three shawls around her shoulders. The fact that she was perspiring profusely didn't seem to bother her. Next, she took out all the jewelries and wore them one by one. The jewelry items were mostly necklaces and bangles. They were cheap, one could tell, though fancy-looking. She might have picked them at some souvenir shop to give away as gifts to friends and relatives. With layered clothes, and necklaces that almost covered her breasts, she trudged toward the weighing machine, again, rolling her suitcase behind her.

When she placed the suitcase on the weighing machine, with fury written all over her face, the lady from Ryanair couldn't help laughing. When the lady nodded her head, meaning the weight was within the permissible limit, the Turkish woman let out a heavy sigh and threw a nasty look at her. Other passengers who had been watching the scene burst out laughing. Paying no attention to their reaction, she trudged back to her seat. Hardly had she plumped herself on the seat when an announcement came from Ryanair, asking all passengers to proceed to the check-in counter.

Sitting next to me on my flight from Frankfurt to Oslo were two South Asian-looking girls. When they started speaking in Urdu, I asked them whether they were from Pakistan or India. "Our parents came from Pakistan," the older of the two replied. "We were born and brought up in Oslo."

They were college students, ages 19 and 21, going back to Oslo after visiting their relatives in Frankfurt. Both were wearing jeans and T-shirt. The only thing Muslim about their appearance was the headscarf each was wearing.

"Are you happy in Norway?" I asked them.

"Yes," the older one said. "Norway is our home. We are part of the second-generation Pakistanis living in Norway."

"We have relatives all over Europe," the younger one added. "We visit them, especially in the summer."

"Do you speak Norwegian as well as you speak English?" I asked.

"Yes," she said. "At college, the medium of instruction is Norwegian. English is taught as a second language and it is compulsory. With non-Norwegian students, we always speak in English. At home we speak Urdu. So we are comfortable in three languages."

"Are you familiar with Oslo?" I asked her. Showing her the address of the hostel where I would be staying, I added, "Do you know how far this place is from the airport?"

"We don't know Oslo that well," she said. "Our dad is a taxi driver. He will know. He is coming to pick us up. You can ask him."

The two Pakistani sisters made my flight from Frankfurt to Oslo a pleasant experience. We continued our conversation, at the arrival section, while waiting for our bags at the carousel. Their only regret, they said, was that they were not able to visit their relatives in Pakistan as often as they wanted to. "Our dad can't afford it," the older one said. "We have visited our parents' homes in Karachi only twice."

When our bags arrived, I saw the younger one experiencing difficulty in picking up her bag with one hand. Her other hand was already wheeling her cabin bag. I offered to help and grabbed the bag from the carousel. While walking toward the exit, with two sisters on either side, I couldn't help thinking: "How proud I would be, if I had daughters like these two!"

The happy feeling vanished the moment I saw a middle-aged man come out of a car parked near the exit door, looking furious.

"Uh-oh, am I in trouble?" I said to myself. His baggy pajamas and a kurta that reached almost up to his ankles, along with a thick mustache to match, put him in a world entirely different from that of his jeans-and-T-shirt-clad daughters. I was nervous when I went up to him for a handshake. He did shake hands with me all right, but with no letup in the fury on his face.

"Your daughters told me that you might be familiar with this address," I said, showing him the printout of my hostel-booking.

He took a look at it and told me which bus to catch. Pointing at a nearby bus-stop, he added, "That's where you get your bus." He was quite matter-of-fact and the fury on his face was still intact.

I thanked him, smiled at the girls – I dared not shake hands with them – and walked away. The sweet disposition of the two girls and the rude behavior of their father offered a study in contrast. "Or was it the natural reaction of a father who saw his daughters rubbing shoulders with a total stranger?" I tried to reason.

Sri Lankan Tamils Perk Me Up

The hostel I ended up in was a disaster. It was the gloomiest hostel I have ever stayed in during my travels around the world all these years. This was my second visit to Oslo. On my last visit, I had made the mistake of arriving in the city without any hotel or hostel reservation. The only vacant room I could find, that too after a long wandering that followed an all-night train journey, was an attic, at a price that was beyond my budget. This time, I had booked a bed in a hostel several days in advance. To fit my budget, I had picked a hostel a few miles away from the city proper.

It fit the budget all right, but was located in a desolate area. I was feeling depressed as I approached the hostel's main gate, but the *"enna ayya?"* greeting from three South-Indian-looking young men who came out of the gate perked me up. I knew that they used the Tamil equivalent of "What's up?" to greet me because they took me for a fellow Tamil.

When they said that they were from Sri Lanka, I saved them the trouble of narrating to me the story of how they ended up in Norway. I had heard stories and stories of how the Tamil victims of Sri Lanka's quarter-century-long civil war ended up in various European cities. The three had just finished their day shift at the hostel and were going out for a stroll. They worked at the hostel as room-cleaners. I was saddened to hear that all three were college graduates who had worked as clerks in government offices back in Sri Lanka.

"Hang in there," I told them. "This country has a very humane policy toward those who flee persecution in their home countries. I am sure you will make it here." I shook hands with each and wished them "all the best."

"Thank you, sir," all of them said and continued their stroll.

At the hostel's reception desk, I had a funny exchange with the Albanian receptionist. In the form he handed me to fill out, there was a line that read "Date of Labor." I asked him, "Do you think I came here with labor pain?"

"It means your date of birth, sir," the receptionist said.

"What if the mother was in labor for more than a day?" I said. "Which date do you give – the date on which the labor pain started or the date on which it ended?"

The receptionist laughed. "You are not the first one amused by this," he said. "I think the hostel made a mistake when it printed the form the first time and never bothered to correct it."

"No," I told him. "I think there is more to it. I think it has some religious or cultural connotation. It is worth exploring."

"Enjoy your stay, sir," he said, handing me the key to the room.

To my delight, I found that one of the three persons I would be sharing the room with was an Indian. He was from the southern Indian state of Tamil Nadu. He had just completed his master's in electrical engineering from a Norwegian university and landed a job at an IT firm. "Before taking up the job, I decided to do a bit of traveling," he said.

"That's a very good decision," I told him. "Most of my Indian engineer friends in the U.S. are products of IITs. Did you complete your bachelor's at one of those IITs?"

"No," he said. "I completely skipped the Indian Institute of Technology route. I did my undergraduate and graduate studies in Norway. I got a Norwegian government scholarship that took care of all expenses, both tuition and boarding."

"In your case, you didn't cost India anything. That's not the case with those IIT graduates who are now in the U.S. They went to the U.S. for higher studies and then decided to stay on. It was easy for them to make that decision because a degree from IIT is much valued in the American job market. The loser is India, which had spent a fortune on their education."

We talked for a few more minutes – about other things that were happening in India, about his experience in Norway as a student, about how I ended up in Norway, and so on.

When I found that I had no more energy left to stay awake, I excused myself, saying, "I had a long day and have several hours' sleep to catch up with."

After a quick shower, I hit the bed. In a few seconds, I was fast asleep.

31

Cruising through Oslo Fjord, and by Quisling's House

August 12, 2009 – Wednesday

One of the disappointments I had, after my visit to Norway in 2008, was that I didn't have a chance to take a fjord cruise the country is famous for. "Frankly," says Rick Steves, the famous travel writer, "if you go to Oslo and don't get out to the fjords, you should have your passport revoked." I took it as an admonition of Oslo visitors like me. The cruise that Steves strongly recommends is the one through Sognefjord. It's the longest (120 miles) and deepest (more than a mile) fjord in Norway.

Another person who drove home to me the importance of taking a fjord cruise while in Norway was a young lady from Washington, D.C., whom I had run into during my 2008 visit. I was on my way from Oslo to Bergen by train. When I saw her and several other passengers get off the train at a station called Myrdal, I asked her what was so important about that station. "Are you planning to do anything interesting here?"

"Don't you know?" she replied. "This is where the Flam Railway begins. From here, I take a train to Flam. From Flam, I go on a sightseeing cruise through the famous Aurlandsfjord."

Last time, it was lack of planning that denied me the pleasure of either the Sognefjord cruise recommended by Rick Steves or the Aurlandsfjord cruise that a lady went all the way from Washington to take. This time, it was shortage of funds. I was on a tight budget. Still, because a fjord cruise had become an obsession with me, I was determined to take at least one that would fit my budget and available time. After a quick breakfast at the hostel, I took a bus to the Oslo harbor, the starting point for all kinds of cruises.

As the bus passed by the marinas, I was awestruck by the number of boats docked there. There were thousands of them, and they came in various sizes and shapes. Most of them were sailboats. There were some fishing boats too. One of the travel brochures I had picked up at the hostel said that every fifth Norwegian owned a boat. Which means that, at any given time, there are one million boats either docked in Norway's marinas or sailing around. Sailing is a favorite pastime among Norwegians. They sail far away from the shore to enjoy swimming, sunbathing and fishing. Fishing is also the second-largest industry in Norway, the first being the oil industry.

I could also see, off the shore, huge oceangoing cruise ships, some anchored and others arriving and departing. During the tourist season, the Oslo harbor handles about 150 international cruise ships.

At the harbor, there were numerous kiosks that sold tickets for all kinds of cruises. One that displayed a colorful banner, with "Batservice Sightseeing A.S." written on it, caught my attention. I bought a ticket for a two-hour cruise that would go through the Oslo Fjord and around some of the beautiful islands, and promised a "spectacular view of the city from the water." I found the price of 250 Norwegian kroner for a two-hour cruise reasonable, given that everything in Norway was expensive.

There were about 100 tourists on the boat. The main tour guide was an attractive young woman with a slight British accent. When I asked her how she got that accent, she said, "I am very much a Norwegian. My three-year stay in London might have corrupted my accent. I am studying for my master's in business at the London School of Economics. I come home every summer and work for this company."

Her beauty and sense of humor were matched by her knowledge as a tour guide. She could effortlessly rattle off facts and figures from Norway's history and politics. She gave brief descriptions of the castle and fortress the boat passed by. Surprisingly, she added, they survived all the wars Norway participated in.

Of the museums the boat passed by, the guide mentioned two in particular: the Kon-Tiki Museum and the Norwegian Folk Museum. "Unfortunately, this tour package doesn't include any museum visit," she said. "But if you have some free time, do visit at least these two. You will learn a lot about Norway's past history."

We also passed by some dilapidated boats, reminders of Norway's Viking past. According to the guide, the Vikings used those boats in the explorations and plunders they were engaged in from the eighth to tenth century. The boats now serve as museum pieces.

Pointing to some of the summer houses almost jutting into the water, the guide said that a 1960 Norwegian law prohibited building houses so close to the water. Those built before the law was passed were allowed to stand. The guide also said the names of those who owned some of the expensive houses and islands.

When the boat passed by the house once owned by the late Vidkun Quisling, she took a few extra minutes to explain how the word "quisling" entered the English lexicon as a synonym for "traitor." I whispered into her ear that European colonialists ruled India as long as they did because they succeeded in converting many Indians into quislings. "Every European colony had some of them," she whispered back.

As the cruise was winding down, I thanked her "for the great time" I had. "Your knowledge of world history and politics is very impressive," I added.

When I suggested that she pose with me for a picture, she

My Thirty-Day European Odyssey

said it would cost me money. "Just kidding," she hastened to add, as she stood by my right side, ready for the picture.

"What about me?" her friend and coworker on the boat, equally attractive, asked.

"Of course, you can join us," I told her, grabbing her hand and pulling her toward my left side. "We'll make it a threesome."

A fellow tourist, who had been watching us, volunteered to take our picture and took my camera from me. "Make it look really good," the tour guide said. "The picture is going all the way to India."

After thanking the man who took the picture, I turned to the guide and said, "There is nothing unusual about your demanding that you be paid for posing for pictures. Those girls in New York's Times Square make a fortune every summer posing for pictures with tourists. But they do it wearing nothing more than a thong underwear. Elegant tour company uniform, like the one you are wearing, may not entice men."

"I think I will keep this job," the guide said.

"I don't doubt it for a moment," I told her and gave her a hug.

At the end of the cruise, I once again approached her. "In my years of travel, I have found Norway to be the most expensive country in the world," I told her. "Every time I shelled down money for a product or service in Norway, I did it grudgingly. Not this time. Your company has earned every one of the 250 kroner charged for this cruise."

The guide grinned. "Thank you, sir," she said. "Thank you for those kind words. I am glad you enjoyed our service."

The place where our cruise ended – Pipervika in central Oslo – was teeming with tourists. It's close to many important landmarks like the Royal Palace, Karl Johans Gate, the Oslo Cathedral and the Ibsen Museum. I had wandered around the area during my 2008 visit. As I was in familiar territory, and as the evening was still young, I decided to do some wandering this time also.

I once again ended up on Karl Johans Gate, the very first

street I walked on during my 2008 visit. This for-pedestrians-only street stretches all the way to the Royal Palace. Both the street and the palace owe a great deal to Karl Johan (king of Sweden from 1818 to 1844): the former was named after him and the latter began its construction, in 1825, on his initiative. The construction was completed in 1848 by King Oscar I. Both Karl Johans Gate and the Royal Palace are also reminders of the nine-decade-long union that existed between Sweden and Norway. It was an unhappy union that came to an end in 1905, when Norway unilaterally declared its independence from Sweden.

Walking toward the Royal Palace, looking at the park to my left, I remembered the pleasant conversation I had with an elderly Norwegian, during my last visit. He had been sitting on a bench, watching me photograph the statue of Henrik Wergeland. Thanks to my conversation with him, I learned what place Henrik Wergeland occupies in Norway's history. Another surprising element in that conversation was that the man turned out to be very knowledgeable about Indian history too. He was an admirer of Mahatma Gandhi.

Protest against Ahmadinejad

Little did I know, when I started walking on Karl Johans Gate, that there was a pleasant surprise waiting for me this time too. This time, it came in the form of a protest by a bunch of Iranian exiles living in Oslo. They were protesting against human rights violations committed by Iranian President Mahmoud Ahmadinejad, and demanding democracy in Iran. More than his human rights violations and anti-democratic actions, it was his persistent Holocaust-denying pronouncements that earned him notoriety in the West.

"Demokrati for Iran," read some of the placards held up by the demonstrators. There were about 100 of them. I had a chat with one of the organizers of the protest. According to her, there are over 11,000 Iranians living in Norway. Most of them live in Oslo.

"I am sure," I told her, "your compatriots back home would be proud of what you are doing here on their behalf. Back home, they will be able to do it only at the risk of being imprisoned."

"Yes, some of my friends are already in prison," she said.

"Do you know what my favorite *New York Times* columnist Maureen Dowd calls President Ahmadinejad?" I asked her.

"No, I don't."

"She calls him Iamadinnerjacket."

She laughed loudly, and then added, "That's too much of a compliment for Ahmadinejad. He stinks."

I wished her and her fellow demonstrators "all the best," and continued my wandering.

It was 8 p.m., and I was tired and hungry. The nearest bus-stop, where I could catch a bus going in the direction of my hostel, was in front of the central train station. I walked in that direction.

At the train station, there were many fast-food places. I decided to pick up something at one of them so I could eat it at the hostel later. To my delight, I saw, at the very entrance to the station, an eatery that had Indian dishes displayed on its menu board. The place happened to be Nepali-owned. The prices of the dishes were reasonable by Norwegian standards. It had been a few days since I had any Indian food. So I had no hesitation in shelling down a little over 11 U.S. dollars for an order of chicken curry and rice.

The food was very tasty.

32

The More I Travel, the More I Discover My Ignorance

August 13, 2009 – Thursday

I was passing by the Oslo City Hall. In Oslo, a city reputed for its modern architecture, this building is acclaimed to be one of its "architectural gems." It is home to the Oslo City Council and numerous galleries and studios. The city hall's reputation can also be attributed to its association with the Nobel Peace Prize. The annual prize-giving ceremony is held in this building.

"But that takes place only on December 10," I said to myself, noticing some hectic activities going on inside the building. "Today is August 13. What could be happening there now?"

I decided to go in and find out.

But the guard at the gate wouldn't let me in. "Not now, sir," he said. "Right now, the City Council is discussing some important legislation. It will be put to vote soon. Unless you have an appointment with someone inside at this time, I can't let you in. Even organized tours are not allowed now."

He told me that the best way to see and learn about everything inside was to join one of the organized tours. "Some of the tours are free," he added.

I thanked him for the information. "Time permitting," I told him, "I may join one of the tours later."

There were plenty of things around, which any visitor to the area would find amusing and educative. One doesn't have to be an art aficionado to appreciate the aesthetic quality of the sculptures and other artworks outside the city hall. None would fail to notice the marble sculpture, featuring a naked woman and her two naked kids. All three are mounted on a high pedestal in the middle of a few fountains. They are presented as though the kids are about to jump off the pedestal and the mother is preventing them from doing it. She is shown holding their hands firmly.

"If the front of the woman is this revealing, what would her behind be like?" I said to myself as I went to the opposite side. To my surprise, what I saw was the front of another naked woman, but holding the hands of the same kids.

A man standing nearby had been watching the statues as amusedly as me. "It's a lovely piece of art," I told him. "There is no doubt about it. Do you know whether it has any other significance?"

"I am a Norwegian," he said, "and I am supposed to know. But I am ashamed to say I don't."

"Don't be ashamed," I said. "There are many things in my country which tourists from around the world come to see. Many of them have historical and spiritual significance. But I know nothing of them. I have an appropriate title for this work of art: *Kids with Two Moms*."

"Not unusual in this day and age," he replied.

Two women who were passing by overheard our conversation. "Call it *A Naked Family*," one of them said.

"*A Naked Family*! That's even better," I told her. "You must get it copyrighted and sell it to the Oslo city administration. You can make some money." She laughed away my suggestion.

Exhibition on the Sidewalk

I was walking in the direction of the waterfront when an exhibition on the sidewalk caught my attention. The exhibits were photographs taken by one Bard Loken. He had permission from the city administration to hold the exhibition on the sidewalk, so close to the city hall. In choosing the sidewalk, rather than a rented gallery, to present his works, he was sparing the public a few Norwegian kroner. Everything in Norway is expensive.

The photographs on display, as their captions said, had been taken by Loken with a view to interpreting "ten commissioned industrial sites in the country. He traveled with his camera from Melbu in the north to Sjolingstad in the south." The exhibition, entitled "Former Power – New Life: A Meeting Between Industrial Memories and Modern Times," was organized by an architect called Julia Yran.

In a few more minutes I was on the waterfront. Prosperity was staring at me from everywhere. It was hard to imagine that a little over a century ago, Norway was the poorest of the three Scandinavian countries. Today, it is the richest of the three, and the tenth-richest in the world in terms of per capita GDP. Strolling on the waterfront, enjoying the evening breeze, I took a mental journey through the trials and tribulations that Norway underwent before it reached its present enviable position.

Norway's Transformation

From 1397 until its independence in 1905, Norway's destiny was controlled by its larger and wealthier Scandinavian neighbors, Denmark and Sweden. The three countries were brought under a single administrative authority by the 1397 Union of Kalmar. But Norway, which had suffered heavy losses in population and resources in the mid-14th century bubonic plague, also known as the Black Death, was not treated as an equal partner by the other two. And with Sweden's dropping out of the union, in 1523, it came increasingly under Danish domination. In 1536, it became a province of Denmark.

The Denmark-Norway union also came to an end toward the end of the Napoleonic Wars (1799-1815). Denmark had supported France in those wars. Norway, whose timber had been very much in demand in Western Europe, found itself supporting the shifting alliances that were pitted against France. The other Scandinavian country, Sweden, was part of the anti-France alliances all through the wars. Once the wars ended, with Napoleon's defeat at Waterloo on June 16-17, 1815, the victorious European powers compelled Denmark to sign a treaty ceding Norway to Sweden.

Norway disavowed the treaty – the Treaty of Kiel, as it was called – right away and declared itself an independent kingdom. However, Sweden and the other victors coerced it into accepting the treaty. In return for its cooperation, Norway was promised full autonomy within its boundaries in the Swedish-Norway union.

The Act of Union of 1815 did deliver the promise all right. Norway got its own army, navy, customs and parliament (Storting). Though a modus vivendi prevailed between Norway and Sweden for nine decades, the former resented being lorded over by the latter. The resentment came to a boil on June 7, 1905, when Norway proclaimed its independence from Sweden.

Sweden, angered by the unilateral proclamation, sent its army across the border into Norway. The war between the two, which began on July 26, 1905, lasted until May 17, 1906. It ended when Sweden signed a treaty with Norway – the Treaty of Moss – recognizing the latter's 1905 declaration of independence.

Since then, Norway has been functioning as a fiercely independent country and developing its own characteristic features. The most noticeable feature, lately, has been the humane policy it has adopted toward the less fortunate in the world. Thanks to that policy, Norway has become one of the most sought-after destinations for those fleeing wars, persecution and poverty in their home countries.

Even for those who don't have such problems back home, but just want a better-quality life, Norway has become their preferred destination. It is so ironic that Swedes, who had once treated Norway as an appendage to their country, are now the second-largest immigrant group in Norway.

Its transformation toward becoming the richest Scandinavian country began in 1969, the year in which it discovered oil reserves off its coast and capital began to pour in from abroad.

That transformation is more noticeable in Oslo, which, until a few decades ago, was a sleepy provincial town. The only event of any significance that took place there was the annual ceremony awarding the Nobel Peace Prize. Today, it is the fastest-growing European capital.

Oslo's history dates back to 1050, when the first town-like settlement appeared in the area. It has since undergone several changes, including change in name. After the town was burned down in a devastating fire in 1624, Christian IV, the ruler of Denmark-Norway, built a new one in the area below the Akershus Fortress. He called it Christiania, after him. From 1877 to 1925, Christiania was spelled as Kristiania, following a spelling reform. In 1925, the original name, Oslo, was restored.

Talk with an Icelander

I was in a different world, preoccupied with thoughts on Norway's and Oslo's past, when I noticed a teenage boy and an old woman taking turns in photographing each other, with cruise ships and sailboats in the background. I took the woman to be his grandmother. The confirmation of it came soon after we started talking. "Don't you want a picture of both of you together?" I asked them.

The woman thanked me for the offer and handed me her camera. I snapped a few pictures of them. While handing back the camera, I said, "Let me know whether you like them. Otherwise, I can take some more."

She looked at the pictures and said she liked them. And then she surprised me with the question: "Which part of India are you from?"

"Kerala," I said.

"This is my grandson," she said. "We are from Iceland. My

cousin married a Gujarati forty years ago. Not many marriages in Iceland have lasted that long. They seem to be happily married."

"Where did they meet?" I asked her.

"In Iceland," she said. "He had come to Reykjavik to study engineering. He met my cousin at the university. She is also an engineer. Both are retired now. They spend their retirement between Spain, where they have built a house, and Reykjavik."

I couldn't resist bringing up the bankruptcy Iceland's economy had suffered a couple of months earlier. It had wiped out the entire lives' savings of many Icelandic families. "Were you hurt too?" I asked her.

Not that she showed any signs of privation. She was elegantly dressed and bubbling with energy and enthusiasm.

"Our country has gone through worse," she said. "We'll weather this one also."

"I am sure you will," I said.

Shaking hands with her and her grandson, I said, "Please convey my congratulations to your cousin and her Indian husband for making their marriage a success. Not many intercontinental marriages have lasted as long as theirs. Your cousin-in-law has done India proud."

That was the last of the memorable conversations I had with total strangers during my month-long wanderings in Europe.

Conversations like this, and the events and objects I got exposed to, during my travels have made an invaluable addition to my knowledge of, and perspective on, the world and its peoples. They have also served as reminders to me that what I have learned so far is only a fraction of what I have yet to do. "The more I travel, the more I discover my ignorance," I keep saying to myself, mangling the immortal words of Percy Shelley, the 19th-century English poet.

Shelley's oft-quoted immortal words are: "The more we study, the more we discover our ignorance."

PICTURES

1
Once a Navy Ship, Now a Youth Hostel

The af Chapman, a full-rigged steel ship. Originally called *Dunboyne* and launched in February 1888, it made several voyages between Europe, Australia and the west coast of America. The Swedish Navy bought it in 1923 and named it after the shipbuilder and Vice Admiral Fredrik Henrik af Chapman. It remained part of the Swedish Navy until its retirement in 1947. After its retirement, the Stockholm City Museum saved it from being dismantled. Permanently moored at the western shore of Skeppsholmen islet in Stockholm, it is now part of the af Chapman youth hostel. Rooms on the ship are more expensive than those in the shore section of the hostel. Though expensive, they get sold out faster because of its locale: The ship floats on placid waters and, when viewed from the shore, has Stockholm's famed Old Town (the Gamla Stan) and the Royal Palace in the background.

2

Monument to Birger Jarl

This cenotaph of Birger Jarl, at the Stockholm City Hall, is cast in bronze, with gold coating. It shows Birger Jarl lying on an empty golden tomb. A visitor is reminded of the statue of the Buddha in the famous Buddha temple in Bangkok. One of the differences is that in the Bangkok temple, the Buddha is shown lying on his side, relaxing. Here, Birger Jarl is shown dead, lying on his back. The most important difference is that while the Birger Jarl monument is gold-plated, the Buddha statue is made of solid gold. Tons of it.

3

Changing of the Guard at Sweden's Royal Palace

Tourists watching the Changing of the Guard ceremony, at the Royal Palace, Stockholm. For many tourists, this spectacular show is one of the reasons why they visit the palace.

4

A Cruise Ship Leaving the Stockholm Harbor

The author on an evening stroll in the Old Town (Gamla Stan) area of Stockholm. Seen in the background is a luxury cruise ship leaving the Stockholm harbor.

5
The Lutheran Cathedral, Helsinki

The Lutheran Cathedral, Helsinki. This imposing structure in Senate Square was built over a period of 22 years, from 1830 to 1852. It underwent some renovation in 1998. Today, it is one of the most popular tourist sites in the Finnish capital, receiving more than 350,000 visitors a year.

6

The Statue of Three Blacksmiths

The Statue of Three Blacksmiths, in Helsinki. It was donated to the city by the Pro Helsingfors Foundation, in 1932. According to a story the Finns enjoy telling visitors, the blacksmiths strike the anvil with their hammers whenever a virgin walks by. No such striking happened when the author saw a few teenage girls pass by. Which made him ask his Finnish friend, "Does it mean that not one of these girls is a virgin?"

7
Statue of Havis Amanda

The statue of *Havis Amanda*, in Helsinki. This nude female statue was sculpted in Paris, in 1906, by Ville Vallgren and erected in Helsinki's Market Square on September 20, 1908. The statue depicts a mermaid standing on seaweed and surrounded by four sea lions, with four fish spouting water at her feet. The model for the statue, according to sculptor Vallgren, was a 19-year-old Parisian by the name of Marcelle Delquini. Vallgren's preferred title for his artwork was *Merenneito* (The Mermaid). But newspapers dubbed it *Havis Amanda*, and travel guides and brochures popularized it. That's how the title *Havis Amanda* got stuck. In the beginning, the work had drawn a lot of criticism, especially from women's rights groups. Some women said that the naked woman in the work looked like "a common French whore." Thanks to a small group of Finnish-Swedish supporters, the work gradually gained widespread acceptance. Today, many consider it "the most important and most beautiful piece of art in Helsinki." There are men who believe that washing the face with the water from one of *Havis Amanda*'s fountains and shouting *"Rakastaa"* (approximate translation: "I love you") three times increases the libido.

8

The Winter Palace, St. Petersburg

The author in front of the Palace Square entrance of the Winter Palace, St. Petersburg. The two incidents that changed the course of Russia's history forever, the "Bloody Sunday 1905" and the October 1917 Bolshevik coup, occurred here – the former, outside the palace gate; and the latter, inside the palace. Today, the Winter Palace is part of the Hermitage Museum, one of the largest in the world. It gets 2.5 million visitors a year.

9

The Alexander Column in St. Petersburg

The Alexander Column in Palace Square, St. Petersburg. It gets its name from Czar Alexander I, who ruled Russia from 1801 to 1825. It was built as a monument to his victory over Napoleon in the 1812 war. Seen in the background is the General Staff Building, which headquartered the Imperial Army General Staff in czarist days and now houses different government offices.

10

The Catherine Palace, Pushkin

A bird's-eye view of the Catherine Palace and the surrounding gardens, at Pushkin, a beautiful suburb of St. Petersburg. *(The picture is reproduced courtesy st.petersburg.com)*

11

The Samson Fountain at Peterhof

The Samson Fountain and the Sea Channel in the Peterhof complex. The fountain, showing water spouting from the mouth of a lion ripped open by Samson, represents the biblical story of Samson defeating the lion. It symbolizes Russia winning over Sweden in the Great Northern War. The Samson Fountain and the Sea Channel stretching all the way up to the Gulf of Finland are among the major attractions of Peterhof, St. Petersburg.

12

Kazansky Cathedral, St. Petersburg

The Kazansky Cathedral, St. Petersburg. It was built between 1801 and 1811. Emperor Paul I, who ordered its building, wanted it to look like St. Peter's Basilica in Rome. Though he died on March 23, 1801, those who completed the cathedral's construction did respect his wish. The cathedral's semicircular, colonnaded (it has 96 columns) façade bears evidence to it. It was built to house a copy of an icon of Our Lady of Kazan. One of the stories associated with the cathedral goes thus: When Napoleon's army invaded Russia in 1812, the commander-in-chief of the Russian army, Mikhail Kutuzov, asked Our Lady of Kazan for help. The help did come, and the cathedral became a memorial to the Russian victory over the French. It fell into decline and disrepair in Soviet times. The Communists even converted it into a Marxist museum. Reopened in 1992, after the collapse of communism, it is now one of the leading Russian Orthodox churches in St. Petersburg.

13

An Impromptu Dance Performance

A promising dancer's impromptu performance, at an unremarkable Moscow restaurant. The two-piece band of the restaurant consisted of a keyboard and a guitar. Every time the band played a Russian song, this pretty little thing got up and danced, to the applause of many customers. She did not do it for applause, though.

14

Padlocks of Love on Trees of Love

A "weird Moscow custom": Many newlyweds in the city rush to the Luzhkov Bridge, soon after the wedding ceremony, and hang "Padlocks of Love" on the "Trees of Love" placed on the bridge. Then they throw the keys to the locks into the canal below, thus making their union permanent. According to a joke making the rounds in Moscow, since the practice began, the divorce rate in the city has gone down considerably. The reason? To get a divorce, the couple has to get hold of the key they have thrown into the canal and open the padlock. Many married couples prefer staying married to going through the impossible task of retrieving the keys from the cold, polluted waters of the canal.

15

St. Basil's Cathedral in Red Square

The Cathedral of St. Basil the Blessed in Moscow. This beautiful structure overlooking Red Square was built in 1554-60 by Ivan the Terrible to commemorate his victory over the Tatars of Kazan and Astrakhan. Legend has it that, soon after the building was completed, the Russians blinded the Italian architect who designed it. They did it to prevent him from replicating this architectural wonder elsewhere.

16

The Kremlin Palace Complex

The Kremlin Palace Complex, and the Kremlin Wall on the Moscow River side, as seen from a bridge on the Moscow River. The complex includes the Great Kremlin Palace, built in 1838-49 as the Moscow residence of the czars, and many other structures built before and since. Notable among those 19th century structures is the Armory, connected to the palace by a tunnel. Among the pre-19th century buildings that were incorporated in the complex are the Terem Palace, the Palace of Facets and several old churches. Two Soviet-era additions to the complex are the School for Red Commanders, built in 1932-34, and the Palace of Congresses, built in 1960-61.

17

Tallinn, as Seen from the Cathedral Hill

A panoramic view of Tallinn from Toompea, which is the seat of the government of Estonia. The word Toompea, derived from the German word Domberg, means the Cathedral Hill. It is named after the Aleksandr Nevsky Cathedral. The author is seen here with two local students who were visiting Toompea at the same time as he did.

18

A Monument in Latvian Capital

The monument on the banks of the Daugava River, in the Latvian capital of Riga. It memorializes those killed when police opened fire on a massive rally, on January 13, 1905. The rally was organized by industrial workers and peasants of Latvia to protest the massacre of their brethren that took place in St. Petersburg, Russia, on January 9, 1905. The notorious St. Petersburg incident has been recorded in history as "Bloody Sunday 1905."

19
Warsaw Uprising Memorial

The Warsaw Uprising Memorial in Krasinski Square, Warsaw. The author visited the memorial on August 1, 2009, the 65th anniversary of the uprising, and paid his respects to all Poles who sacrificed their lives in their fight against the Nazis. Many more people came to the site on this day and paid their respects by placing flowers and lighting candles on the steps of the memorial.

20

Stalin's Gift to Polish People

The Palace of Culture and Science or *Palac Kultury i Nauki*, as Poles call it. It was built by 7,000 workers, evenly divided between Soviets and Poles. Though it was supposed to be Stalin's gift to the Polish people, he did not live to see the formal handing over of the gift. Its construction, which began on May 1, 1951, was completed only on July 22, 1955. Stalin died on March 5, 1953.

21

A Panoramic View of Prague

The author, on the Charles Bridge, with a part of Prague in the background. Prague is one of the few cities in Europe that came out of World War II almost intact. The city, with its narrow streets and cobbled passages, reminds one of an older, lost Europe. It has three sections: the Old Town, the Lesser Town and the New Town (*Staré Mesto, Mala Strana* and *Nové Mesto,* respectively, in the Czech language). It has been a place of great architectural and cultural influence since the Middle Ages. Its magnificent monuments, churches and palaces, built mostly in the 14th century by King Charles IV, who was also the Holy Roman Emperor, bear evidence to that fact.

22

Statue of Madonna and St. Bernard on Charles Bridge

This statue of Madonna and St. Bernard, donated in 1709 by Father Benedict, an abbot of the Monastery in Osek, is one of the statues that decorate the Charles Bridge in Prague. Built in the 14th century and named for King Charles IV who ordered its construction, the 1,673-foot-long bridge connecting the Old Town and the Lesser Town of Prague became a piece of art between 1600 and 1800, when "the Catholic desire for ornamentation resulted in 30 statues [of saints] being erected" on it. Now there are 75 statues, but most of them are copies of the original. The originals – those that survived floods and other natural calamities – are now lying in the nearby Czech National Museum.

23

Astronomical Clock in Prague

The Astronomical Clock, which is big tourist draw in Prague. The clock's main attraction is its fascinating mechanical performance every hour, on the hour. At the stroke of every hour, two windows open up on the sides of the clock to reveal 12 apostles greeting the city. Also animated on the sides, on the hour, are a skeleton ringing a bell, a Turk shaking his head, a miser with a bag containing money, and Vanity looking in a mirror. The whole performance ends with the crowing of a golden rooster and the ringing of a huge bell atop the tower. Legend has it that the ghosts and devils flee the city at the first cock-crow in the morning.

24

Wachau Valley, as Seen from Melk Abbey

This panoramic view of the Wachau Valley in Austria, as seen from the Melk Abbey. The scene was captured by the author on his camera when he visited the Abbey in the summer of 2009.

25

Farewell to Friends in Vienna

The author (center) at the central bus station in Vienna on August 8, 2009. He is waiting to take a bus to Bratislava, the capital of Slovakia. With him are his friend Kulamarva Balakrishna (standing) and Balakrishna's wife, Eva. Little did the author know then that it would be his last meeting with Balakrishna. He passed away on February 27, 2013.

26

Frankfurt's Main Train Station

The main train station in Frankfurt. It is said to be the busiest long-distance-train station in Germany, serving over 350,000 travelers a day. On weekdays, it handles 1,800 trains, arriving at and departing from its 24 platforms. The number of trains is slightly smaller on weekends.

27

Euro Symbol, at ECB, Frankfurt

The author standing under the euro symbol, in front of the Eurotower in Frankfurt. The Eurotower houses the European Central Bank (ECB), which administers the policy of the European Monetary Union, also known as the Eurozone. The 12 stars on the euro symbol supposedly represent the number of European Union members that have joined the Eurozone. By the time the author visited Frankfurt, 16 EU members had joined the Eurozone. He was curious to find out whether the number of stars would be increased to 16 soon. "No question from the public is entertained" was the response he received from a guard with intimidating features, who stopped him at the entrance to the ECB.

28

Cruising through the Oslo Fjord

The author, on a cruise through the Oslo Fjord. With him are two employees of the tour company that conducted the cruise. The one to his right is a graduate student at the London School of Economics, who works for the company as a tour guide every summer. Impressed with her knowledge of world history and politics, the author requested, at the end of the cruise, that she pose with him for a picture. "What about me?" the guide's colleague asked. The author dragged her in, saying, "Of course, we'll make it a threesome."

29

Demand for Democracy in Iran

A protest demonstration by Iranian exiles in Oslo, Norway. It was one of the pleasant surprises the author had during his visit to Oslo in the summer of 2009. On August 12, 2009, he saw, during a leisurely walk toward Oslo's Royal Palace, about 100 men and women protesting against human rights violations committed by Iranian President Mahmoud Ahmadinejad, and demanding democracy in Iran. More than his human rights violations and anti-democratic actions, it was his persistent Holocaust-denying pronouncements that earned him notoriety in the West.

30

Statue of 'A Naked Family' in Oslo

This is one of the many sculptures and other artworks that adorn the premises of the Oslo City Hall. Looking at the sculpture, the first question that arose in the author's mind was: "If the front of the woman is this revealing, what would be her behind like?" To find out, he went to the opposite side. What he saw, to his surprise, was the front of another naked woman. That made him come up with an appropriate caption for the artwork: *"Kids with Two Moms."* A woman who overheard him had a better idea. "Call it *A Naked Family*," she said.

www.ingramcontent.com/pod-product-compliance
Lightning Source LLC
Chambersburg PA
CBHW071429070526
44578CB00001B/40